I pity the poor people who don't ride motorcycles.
—Malcolm Smith, champion motorcycle racer

THE Spirit OF THE MOTORCYCLE

THE LEGENDS, THE RIDERS, AND THE BEAUTY OF THE BEAST

By Michael Dregni
Photographs by John Dean
Foreword by Lucky Lee Lott

A TOWN SQUARE BOOK

Voyageur Press
In Cooperation with the Reynolds-Alberta Museum

Edited by Greg Field
Designed by Andrea Rud
Jacket designed by Kristy Tucker
Printed in Hong Kong

oo   o1   o2   o3   o4   5   4   3   2   1

On the endpapers: *1920s Ner-A Car and fan. (Photograph from Frank Westfall/Syracuse Ner-A-Car Museum)*

On the frontispiece, clockwise from top left: *Happy Moto-Scoot rider. The stylish Indian pilot, circa 1922. (Photograph from Provincial Archives of Alberta)*
1918 Henderson Z. Owner: Eldon Brown.

On the title pages: *1942 Indian Sport Scout Model 642. Owner: Eldon Brown.*
Inset on the title page: *Dreaming of big twins, circa 1922. (Photograph from Provincial Archives of Alberta)*

Opposite the contents page: *Flying Merkel advertising poster promoting the motorcycle's latest and greatest feat.*

Library of Congress Cataloging-in-Publication Data
Dregni, Michael, 1961–
    The spirit of the motorcycle : the legends, the riders, and the beauty of the beast / by Michael Dregni ; photographs by John Dean.
        p.   cm.
    "Town Square books."
    Includes bibliographical references and index.
    ISBN 0-89658-450-X
    1. Motorcycling. 2. Motorcyclists. 3. Motorcycles. I. Title.

TL440.5.D74 2000
629.227′5′097—dc21   99-086262

Published by Voyageur Press, Inc.
123 North Second Street, P.O. Box 338, Stillwater, MN 55082 U.S.A.
651-430-2210, fax 651-430-2211

Educators, fundraisers, premium and gift buyers, publicists, and marketing managers: Looking for creative products and new sales ideas? Voyageur Press books are available at special discounts when purchased in quantities, and special editions can be created to your specifications. For details contact the marketing department at 800-888-9653.

ACKNOWLEDGMENTS

I offer my thanks to the following people for their assistance in bringing this book to life.

First my thanks to Rick Budd, Michael Payne, and the staff of the Reynolds-Alberta Museum, photographer John Dean, and the owners of these machines.

In alphabetical order, my thanks to Robert H. Ammon of Cushman; Bruno Baccari; Lindsay Brooke for information on Paul Bigsby and Salsbury; Bob Chantland; Eric Dregni; François-Marie Dumas; Greg Field; Walt Fulton of Mustang; Evel and Kelly Knievel; Lelio Lari; Randy Leffingwell; Lucky Lee Lott; Zachary Miller; Angelo Parrilla; Dr. Martin Jack Rosenblum, Historian at Harley-Davidson; Giuseppe Rottigni of Moto Parilla; E. Foster Salsbury of Salsbury; Fraser Seeley of Fifth House Books; Larry Wise of Cosmopolitan Motors; and Stephen Wright.

Anyone who writes history naturally owes a debt to the historians who came before them, and I am no different. Alongside my interviews and conversations with people directly involved with various motorcycle companies old and new and my own research into archives and magazine and newspaper records, I owe a debt to several of the other historians of the American motorcycle, especially Jerry Hatfield and Allan Girdler. As a motorcyclist, I offer my thanks to them for their work and inspiration.

Finally, my thanks to everyone at Voyageur Press.

Michael Dregni

Movie star Fay Wray of King Kong fame sits asaddle a Harley-Davidson. This image of Wray was taken in 1921 when she was but fourteen years old. (Photograph from Margaret Johnson)

CONTENTS

FOREWORD

By Lucky Lee Lott

For more than two decades, I made my living crashing motorcycles. As the leader of Lucky Lee Lott's Hell Drivers, my boys and I laid to eternal rest 17,981 motorcycles and automobiles at county and state fairs throughout the United States and Canada starting in 1935. Not only did our gasoline opera feature a blood-curdling blend of daredevilry and stunts, the Hell Drivers also destroyed more fine machinery in more imaginative ways than you ever dreamed possible.

Many years before the advent of the motorcycle, the poet Sir Walter Scott framed the words that I have lived by in his poem "The Last Minstrel": "The will to do and the soul to dare." These are words that still dwell in my head at this ripe old age of eighty-four after surviving many a bone-jarring, back-bending, heart-halting motorcycle stunt.

We daredevils were true engineers. In the Hell Drivers, we took pride in crashing motorcycles through brick walls, wooden walls, tin walls, and walls that were set aflame. We drove motorcycles head on into speeding automobiles, jumped from motorcycles onto airplanes at 80 miles per hour, and leaped motorcycles into bodies of water. Daredevilry was a science. It was not foolhardiness or merely the libidinous nature of young men, for broken bones, lacerations, and bruises were not badges of honor among professional daredevils.

Forty years later, I still have fond memories of my signature stunt, the Tin Wall Crash, wherein I piloted a motorcycle through a wall of nothing less than 28-gauge furnace metal. The trick was to fit a sharp blade to the front wheel's fender and stake down the tin wall as taut as possible. Then I just gassed the throttle, aimed straight, and ducked my head. Back in those days, we wore football helmets to keep our craniums in one piece.

I also parlayed my knack of crashing motorcycles into a sideline career as a movie stunt man—"fall guys," as we called them for obvious reasons. I did my bit in Marlon Brando's *The Wild One* as well as many other movies. Guys who could crash cycles and cars without getting hurt and running up the hospital bill were in demand in Hollywood.

In my days of daredevilry, I naturally had my favorite cycles. I remained true to Nash automobiles, which was our sponsor throughout the 1940s and 1950s. But in terms of cycles, different machines did different jobs. I always loved a Harley-Davidson and favored our good, solid Henderson Four for our Head-On Crash. We had a couple Ariels—a Red Hunter and Square Four—as well. But there was one machine that stood out, the Indian Scout. It was the daredevil's choice.

I relate this all by way of providing a foreword to my friend Michael Dregni's history of the spirit of motorcycling. From racing to stunt riding, technical developments to transportation evolution, pop culture to outlaw mystique, he tells a good story.

I first worked with Michael in writing and publishing my memoirs of my daredevil days, *The Legend of the Lucky Lee Lott Hell Drivers*. Michael was too young to ride with the Hell Drivers in our glory days but I have christened him an honorary member these days.

Lots of luck,
Lucky Lee Lott
800 East Diana
Tampa, Florida 33605 USA

FLAMING WALL STUNT, 1942
One of Lucky Lee Lott's fearless Hell Drivers blazes through a wall of flames for the cheering crowd at Tremens Circus in the St. Louis, Missouri, Arena. The trick to crashing through a one-inch-thick flaming board wall was to roll the throttle wide open, aim your cycle, and duck your head. A word to the wise: Don't lift your head too soon or you might get a splinter. (Photograph from Lucky Lee Lott Archives)

PREFACE

By Rick Budd, Reynolds-Alberta Museum

The inspiration for this book came from a motorcycle exhibition entitled "Motorcycles Forever" that was organized by the Reynolds-Alberta Museum in 1996. The exhibition will always be regarded by Canadian bike enthusiasts as a remarkable event—at least by all of those who journeyed to Wetaskiwin, Alberta, to see it. Some would even say it was an historic event.

The Reynolds-Alberta Museum (RAM) is a provincially owned and operated facility that was built to showcase an extensive collection of cars, trucks, tractors, steam engines, airplanes, and other forms of machinery, including a handful of American and British motorcycles. When some colleagues and I first started talking about organizing a major motorcycle show, we really had no idea how many older bikes might exist in our part of the world, or whether owners would be willing to lend them for a four-month exhibit.

To get the project rolling, RAM staffer Mike Parsons and I attended a meeting of the Edmonton chapter of the Canadian Vintage Motorcycle Group. Fortunately, our presentation to this club resulted in some knowledgeable members volunteering to help. The project clearly wouldn't have succeeded if not for the generous assistance of Ray Le Blanc, John McEwen, John Oland, Harry Pytel, Byron Reynolds, and Tim Yip. Worthy of special mention is the great success they had in locating significant bikes and coaxing them from the caring hands of their owners. Andy Smith, then an instructor at Alberta's Fairview College, was also a tremendous help—especially when he secured the promise of ten vintage motorcycles from the Trev Deeley Motorcycle Museum in Vancouver. With the exception of this particular loan, all other machines came from individuals.

One by one, desirable bikes were offered, and we began to feel awfully good about the response we were getting. Our search resulted in Canada's oldest operating motorcycle—a 1903 Kerry—being graciously offered by Peter Emmans of Woodstock, Ontario. We were flattered by this loan and many others—including the one from Peter Gagan of White Rock, British Columbia, who overwhelmed us by contributing seven fine machines. While the task of finding pre-1920 bikes looked especially daunting at first, it soon proved otherwise: Important names such as Henderson, Scott, Ariel, Triumph, and Indian were steadily added to the exhibit's lineup. Within a few months, loans of more than a hundred motorcycles were confirmed and shipping arrangements were being made with nearly fifty owners in British Columbia, Alberta, Saskatchewan, and Ontario, and one contributor from Washington.

"Motorcycles Forever" jolted the senses of everyone interested in vintage iron. Even non-motorcyclists were impressed. The bikes—whether beautifully restored or purposely kept in original condition—prompted reactions that ranged from long silent stares to animated discussion. Faces glowed with excitement, eyes misted over, voices became spiked with emotion, and heads nodded with approval.

The exhibit benefited from the talents of many individuals. There are far too many people to mention by name, but each of them can feel proud of their involvement as they browse through this book and recall the days when "Motorcycles Forever" enjoyed the spotlight. It was an exhibition that needed to be done, and done well. Hats off to all!

Nearly 60,000 visitors saw the exhibition during

1948 INDIAN CHIEF
The quintessential motorcycle. Owner: Dave Martin.

the summer of 1996, but we always knew that a much larger audience would appreciate seeing these bikes. So, we began to look for a publisher. When we sent samples of John Dean's exquisite photographs to Michael Dregni at Voyageur Press, it didn't take long before details of this book were being worked out and more motorcycle images were being requested. This led to other photo sessions in 1997 after I tracked down specific bikes that weren't in the exhibition. In Calgary, John and I set up numerous shots in the workshop of Harley-Davidson of Southern Alberta, followed by others inside the Site Oil Tools plant. Our work continued in Prince George, British Columbia, where Eldon Brown—who had loaned four superb machines to the exhibition—and his father Carman Brown welcomed us into their restoration shop to select and photograph vintage American bikes from their impressive collection.

The Reynolds-Alberta Museum is grateful to author Michael Dregni for his personal commitment to this project. Without him, our motorcycle images might now be sitting somewhere in a storage cabinet instead of being enjoyed by thousands. Needless to say, we're glad the photos attracted his attention, and that this book was given the green light by his colleagues at Voyageur Press. It is satisfying that this publication extends the reach of our temporary exhibition. Indeed, *The Spirit of the Motorcycle* resonates with the collective passion of enthusiasts on both sides of the border.

Rick Budd
Reynolds-Alberta Museum,
Alberta Community Development

PROUD THIEM OWNER, 1915
The Thiem Manufacturing Company of St. Paul, Minnesota, offered its side-valve, 31-ci (508-cc), single-cylinder motorcycle in 1912. The firm also built motorcycle engines and complete machines that were sold by other firms under different names.

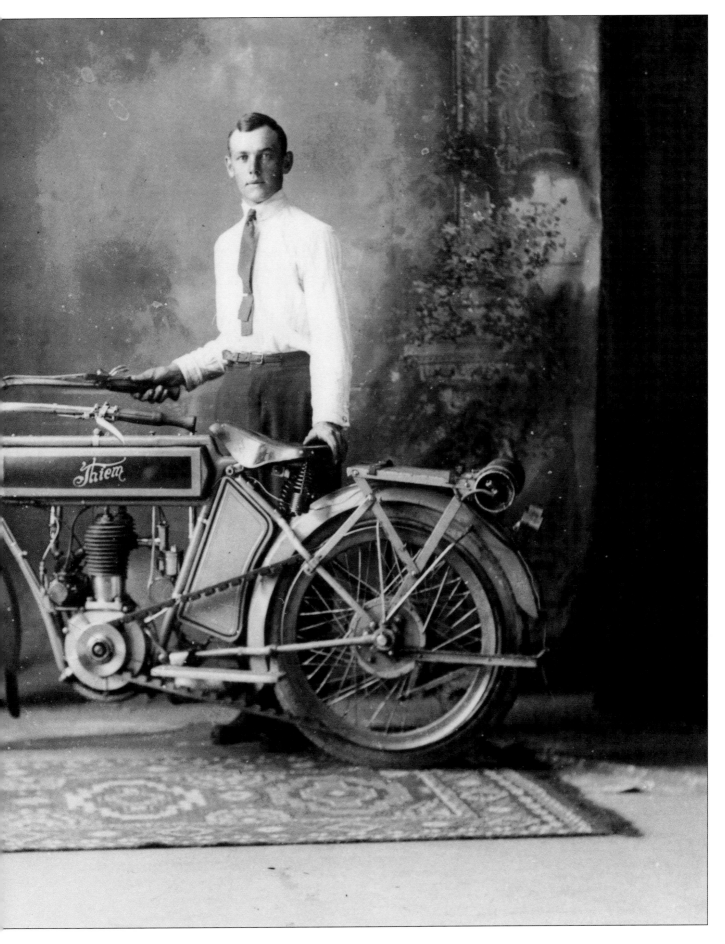

PREFACE

By Michael Dregni

My fascination with the history of motorcycles began with the Cyclone, which seems as fine a place as any other to start. I can date my interest to an autumn day a decade or so ago when I was first shown an actual Cyclone engine by Bob Chantland, who had come across the dismantled motor in a typical basket of miscellaneous spare parts. The beauty of that engine was astonishing and led me to begin researching the Cyclone, just as Bob was also doing. To my pleasant surprise, I found that I was then living just blocks from the old Cyclone factory in St. Paul, Minnesota, and its main battleground, the Twin City Motordrome. I had been riding Lambretta and Vespa motorscooters and Parilla, BMW, and Ducati motorcycles for years, but the vision of the Cyclone was something new. Here was a machine built figuratively in my own backyard, with a heroic history that had all the elements of myth and legend.

During all of the years I have spent wrenching and riding on motorcycles, I have always collected stories, photographs, brochures, and memorabilia. Along with the machines themselves, these artifacts served as mnemonics, a way to keep memories and history alive. I guess it is only natural that they form the backbone of a book.

This volume makes no pretense of being a true history of motorcycles, full of important dates, essential facts, and details of model evolution. It is also not a coffee-table gallery of motorcycles as static art. It is designed instead to be a history of people and motorcycles; if it has to be labeled, I would term it a cultural or sociological history.

Instead of following a strict chronology of events, I have focused on themes that have formed motorcycling, events that have shaped the sport, and people who built and rode cycles—some of whom have become legends, others who have been largely forgotten by history. For example, instead of providing a timeline of how motorcycle racing developed in the United States and who won what race by how many tenths of a second, I have chosen instead to tell the story of the fabulous Cyclone motorcycle and its times. And instead of giving annual sales figures and comparisons to explain the invasion of the North American market by European and Japanese motorcycles, I have chosen to chronicle three incidents that occurred as part of the invasion. I believe the Cyclone's tale illustrates the spirit of racing, and these other stories bring the past alive in our memories much better than any statistical analysis could.

All of this explanation is not to say that this is a better way to write a book or that this book is better than any motorcycling histories that have come before it. There's a time-place for all types of books, from the model development history to the cultural history. To me, motorcycles are an alchemy of metal and fire, but it is the people who build and tune and ride them that give the machines life. This is simply the only way I know how to write this book.

In the end, please accept this book for what it is rather than what it is not. If this book resurrects some memories, revives some ghosts, and makes you want to go out and ride, then I call it a success.

Michael Dregni

1936 UNO-WHEEL

The Uno-Wheel aimed to defy the laws of balance. Farsighted engineering savant Walter Nilsson began work in 1926 to create the perfect motor-driven single-wheeler. Powered by a 12-hp, single-cylinder engine and driven via a three-speed gearbox, the unicycle cavorted down the road at speeds of up to 100 mph (161 kph). The main drawback to the Uno-Wheel was the cost of the specially made tire: 5-feet-by-3-inch (120x7.5-cm) tires were not available at your local dealer—then or now—and cost Nilsson a cool $800. Fortunately, he only needed one.

Chapter 1

IRON HORSES

PIONEERING MOTORCYCLES AND MANUFACTURERS

"IT BEATS THE OLD WAY," 1904

ABOVE: *The first motorcycles were simply bicycles mounted with one of the newfangled internal-combustion engines. Thus, it was little wonder that the first advertisements for machines like the Merkel from the O. Merkel Manufacturing Company of Milwaukee, Wisconsin, touted their advantages over the old-fashioned leg-powered bicycles. As this 1904 ad promised: "You don't work while you ride."*

1868–1869 ROPER STEAMER

LEFT: *Sylvester H. Roper of Roxbury, Massachusetts, was a brave man. He crafted this steam-powered, wooden-framed velocipede in 1868–1869 and set forth onto the roads around Boston—where he was quickly arrested by the vigilant keepers of law and order. Thus, Roper may be not only heralded as one of the pioneer motorcycle builders but also branded as the first motorcycle outlaw. (Courtesy of the Smithsonian Institution, NMAH/Transportation. Photograph by Jeff Tinsley)*

Horse manure. It was a sign of the times, the byproduct of the chief mode of transportation and motive power of the 1800s, the horse. Before the days of steam or the internal-combustion engine, horses—as well mules, asses, oxen, and other drayage animals—provided the power that propelled the world's economies. By the 1890s, the United States boasted 27 million horses that were saddled with myriad tasks, from powering farm implements to towing canal boats and from hauling freight carts to pulling carriages on the avenue. In fact, horse power was so prevalent that it became a standard measurement for energy and work. But just as engine exhaust fumes curse our air today, horse manure was a malodorous fact of everyday life in the nineteenth century.

In New York City alone, horses produced on average 500 tons (454 tonnes) of manure daily in the 1890s. In October 1899, the first issue of the fledgling *Automobile Magazine* bemoaned streets that were "literally carpeted with a warm, brown matting of comminuted horse dropping, smelling to heaven and destined in no inconsiderable part to be scattered in fine dust in all directions, laden with countless millions of disease breeding germs." Among these germs was tetanus, and the dust caused respiratory ailments and bore bacteria that was a source of the dreaded tuberculosis that ravaged people of the day.

Onto these mean streets, negotiating his way through the horses, traffic, and manure, came one Sylvester H. Roper of Roxbury, Massachusetts. Roper rode a home-fashioned contraption that was so novel, so newfangled, so unique that it did not even have a name. While other vehicles were propelled by horse power, Roper had fashioned a new type of "horse" in 1868–1869 that made its own power.

And it did not make manure.

STEAM-POWERED "FAST FEET"

Roper was born in 1823 in Francestown, New Hampshire. During the American Civil War, he was employed at the famed Springfield Armory in Springfield, Massachusetts, where he

COPELAND STEAMER, 1884

In the days when handlebar mustaches were de rigueur, *American visionary Lucius D. Copeland bolted a steam boiler to his handy Star bicycle and created a treacherous-looking high-wheeled motorcycle. Copeland later founded the Motor-Cycle Manufacturing Company of Philadelphia, Pennsylvania, which pioneered the term "moto-cycle."*

lent a hand to perfecting the Spencer repeating rifle and tinkered with steam engines—all state-of-the-art technology for the day. This provided him with experience to fuel an interest in building his self-propelled vehicle, which is believed to be the earliest surviving ancestor of the motorcycle and is today lodged at the Smithsonian Institution's National Museum of American History.

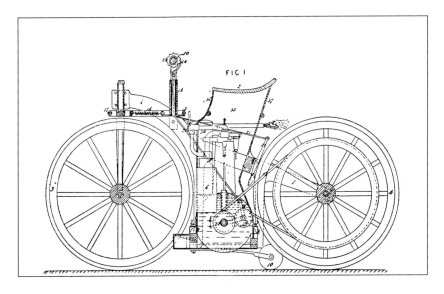

DAIMLER EINSPUR, 1885
German Gottlieb Daimler built a wooden frame around a 16-ci (265-cc), single-cylinder engine to craft what is often crowned as the first gasoline-powered motorcycle. Daimler was wary about taking the first ride on his own creation, however, so he thoughtfully placed his son Paul in the driver's seat for the inaugural outing.

Roper's machine was a wooden, two-wheeled, bicycle-like vehicle powered by a diminutive steam engine. He termed his creation a "steam velocipede" from the Latin word for "fast feet" that was at the time used to describe the pioneering, foot-propelled bicycles. Roper passed out handbills advertising his traveling show, wherein he displayed both his two-wheeler and a pioneering steam-powered four-wheeler, later known to the world at large by the moniker "automobile." Roper billed his show as "The Greatest Mechanical Exhibition in the World." And it probably was at the time.

The wooden frame of Roper's creation followed the style of velocipede frames but appears to have been purpose-built to carry a steam engine. A single backbone ran from the steering head to the engine mounts and back to twin arms that cradled the rear wheel. The steering handlebars with their wooden handgrips were connected to a wrought-iron front fork ending with footrests. Both wheels measured 34 inches (86 cm) in diameter and were fashioned of wood capped by an iron band that served as a "tire." The wheelbase measured 49 inches (124.5 cm).

Roper's miniature steam engine was suspended from the frame in front of the rear wheel. He fed charcoal into the firebox at the base of the boiler through a small round door, and the fire heated water in the boiler into steam. The escaping steam drove pistons in the twin cylinders on each side of the rear wheel; connecting rods on the pistons powered cranks attached to the wheel axle.

Water for the boiler was held in a tank, which doubled as the velocipede's seat. A hand-operated pump forced the water into the boiler, and water-level cocks and a drain helped Roper control the supply. Exhaust steam exited through the cannonlike rear stack. A safety valve allowed steam to escape while the vehicle idled.

In what was perhaps the pioneering use of a twistgrip throttle, the full handlebars themselves controlled the velocipede's speed—as well as its braking. Twisting the handlebars forward operated a throttle on the boiler; twisting them backward applied a friction brake to the front wheel rim.

I wonder who he was? I wish I had a machine like that. I could make better time than I can on my bicycle. Perhaps I'll get one some day.
—Victor Appleton, *Tom Swift and His Motor Cycle*, 1910

DARING YOUNG MAN ON HIS RIDING MACHINE, 1890S

In the brave new world created by the pioneering motorcycles, anything seemed possible when riding one of the gasoline-powered steeds—even this early Evel Knievel–like leap over a picturesque river. This ad for the English Pennington motorcycle was a bravura example of advertising hype.

The world was not ready to climb aboard Roper's invention, although people did pay their hard-earned 25¢ to see Roper ride his self-propelled vehicles at circuses and fairs in Massachusetts and New York. But when Roper went for a ride on his steam velocipede on the streets of Roxbury and Boston, he was soon arrested, branding him the first motorcycle outlaw.

While Roper's creation was innovative for its time, it used available technology, albeit in a novel fashion. Steam power was state of the art for everything from boats to railroad locomotives, so it's not surprising that others were thinking along the same lines as Roper, including the designers of the French Michaux-Perreaux steam-powered velocipede, which also took to the road in 1868–1869. In 1883–1884, American Lucius D. Copeland equipped a Star bicycle with a one-cylinder steam engine and boiler. Copeland's later steamer tricycle became the foundation of the Motor-Cycle Manufacturing Company of Philadelphia, which offered its "Phaeton Moto-Cycle." This fledgling firm pioneered both the name "moto-cycle" and the fate of many such "technology" companies in quickly going nowhere. From today's vantage, however, the surprising thing is not that people fooled with steam power, but that they did not develop it further.

Roper, meanwhile, was still at work. He created another steam velocipede, and on this second-generation velocipede he met his death on June 1, 1896. The seventy-three-year-old Roper was racing the velocipede against bicycles at the Charles River velodrome in Cambridge, Massachusetts. He stoked up the firebox with an extra helping of charcoal, and proceeded to clock a flying mile (1.6 km) at 2:01.4 minutes at a top speed of an astonishing 40 mph (65 kph). Then, as the crowd looked on in horror, Roper's velocipede began to wobble. Roper struggled to control the machine, but he careened off the track and crashed at terrifying speed. Roper's "fast feet" fell silent, and an autopsy blamed Roper's death on a heart attack.

PIONEERING GASOLINE POWER

At the same time as Roper and others were experimenting with steamer "moto-cycles," other inventors were hammering out the details of a new type of engine that was much more compact in size and would thus be more suitable to power a two-wheeler. In 1876, Bavarian inventor Nikolaus August Otto created a motor that formed the foundation for today's four-stroke internal-combustion engine.

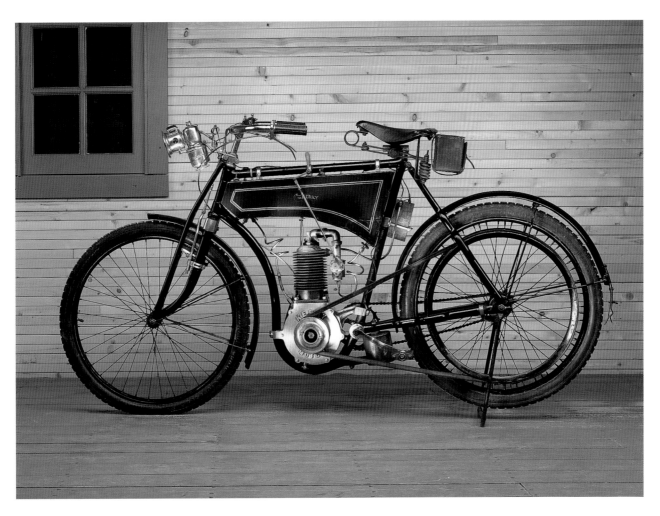

1903 KERRY

Owner Peter Emmans: "Motorcycles like my 1903 Kerry were built with no clutch, gearbox, or springs for comfort. When setting off to ride the Kerry, I must first prime the carb, set the fuel lever, turn on the ignition switch, set the spark lever (advance and retard), then check the road to make sure all is clear. Now I'm ready. If the road is flat and the weather is not too hot, I will start running beside the Kerry, keeping the exhaust valve open by holding the control lever tightly in my left hand. After several steps, I release the lever, and when I hear firing noises I hop on, using the pedals to increase my speed while I feverishly work to set ignition and carb controls and steer, all the while trying to keep my balance. You may say, 'Well, that's not too bad, now the engine is running,' but wait, what about the stop sign, traffic light, or the little old lady crossing in front of me? That's right, no clutch means I have to stop the bike, get off and start all over again.

"On a good road, the Kerry's best speed is 30 mph. While motoring along I must remember to oil the engine every two miles or else it will start making tight noises and get very hot. A few years ago, I rode it a distance of 26 miles in one day and all went well—until the darn rear tire blew. When that happened, I found out what it's like to ride a bucking bronco."

1903 KERRY

Starting around 1902, the East London Rubber Company of London, England, sold the Kerry motorcycle to adventurous souls. The single-cylinder cycles were constructed in Belgium with engines sourced from the famous Belgian armaments maker and motorcycling pioneer Fabrique Nationale (FN). This single displaced 235 cc and drove the rear wheel via a belt with no clutch, as was typical of many early motorcycles. Owner: Peter Emmans.

BICYCLE-TURNED-MOTORCYCLE DEALER, 1900S

ABOVE: *Suddenly bicycles were old hat when the new Indian "moto-cycle" from the Hendee Manufacturing Company of Springfield, Massachusetts, arrived on the scene in 1901. This Minneapolis bicycle dealer shoved his bicycles to the side to display the latest in motorized technology. The Indian was the quintessential motorcycle of the early 1900s with a 15.85-ci (264.2-cc) F-head single-cylinder engine bolted to a modified bicycle chassis. The engine could be throttled back to a walking pace of 3 mph (4.8 kph) or up to a startling full-out dash of more than 30 mph (48 kph)—a heady speed in those days.*

1905 ARMAC

LEFT: *The Armac motorcycle was engineered in 1902 by Archie McCullen in St. Paul, Minnesota, and became a prolific make. Later that same year, Armac production moved to Chicago, Illinois. On this 1905 model, a single-cylinder side-valve engine provided power to the obviously bicycle-based chassis. By the early 1910s, Armac cycles were being sold to Allied Motors Corporation as the AMC and to mail-order retailer Montgomery Ward as the Hawthorne. Allied took over the Armac firm in about 1912 and continued building AMC models until about 1915. Owner: Reynolds-Alberta Museum.*

"GET A HORSE!" 1900S

Public sentiment was none too welcoming when the motorcycle was in its infancy. This 1900s editorial cartoon echoed many folks' view.

It was Germany's Gottlieb Daimler who married Otto's engine with a wooden, bicycle-like vehicle in 1885 to craft what is often crowned as the first gas-powered motorcycle. Daimler used a 16-ci (267-cc) single-cylinder engine that turned at a mere maximum of 700 rpm to father 0.5 hp. When his creation was ready, Daimler set his son Paul off on the *Einspur* (German for "One Track," denoting its two-wheeled, single track) near Stuttgart on November 10, 1885.

By the dawn of the 1890s, motorcycles flourished as other creative minds followed Daimler's lead. In 1894, the German Hildebrand & Wolfmüller partnership launched the world's first production motorcycle. The steel-framed machine was powered by a water-cooled, 91.6-ci (1,500-cc) twin-cylinder engine and rode on Englishman John Boyd Dunlop's new pneumatic rubber tires.

Around the same time, Frenchmen Count Albert de Dion and Georges Bouton crafted a four-stroke single-cylinder of 7.6 ci (125 cc) that created 0.5 hp and ran reliably to 1,800 rpm. Not only was the engine used to power de Dion's own tricycle of the 1890s, but it was also copied near and far, and became one of the most influential early engine designs.

In Paris, the *frères* Werner launched their 1898 *motocyclette* with its single-cylinder engine mounted above, and driving, the front wheel. By 1901, the brothers had reconsidered the front-drive layout and were back with the New Werner, the engine now safely tucked in the frame between the wheels to drive the rear wheel.

In the late 1890s, a budding young machinist in Menomonie, Wisconsin, named Harry Arminius Miller needed a way to get to work. In 1897, Miller used his prodigious machining skills to attach one of the newfangled gasoline engines to a bicycle, rigged up a fuel system and throttle, and had a simple yet efficient personal ride. He then put motorcycles aside and went on to engineer a long lineage of glorious racing automobiles and engines, worked with superchargers, front- and all-wheel drive, and won more than his fair share of U.S. National Championships and Indianapolis 500 races.

In 1897, Louis S. Clarke of Pittsburgh, Pennsylvania, established his Pittsburgh Motor Vehicle Company and crafted his first Autocar tricycle, powered by a single-cylinder gas engine. While Harry Miller had built his motorcycle purely for personal transportation, Clarke had farsighted dreams of manufacturing his Autocar and taking the legwork out of getting about.

By the turn of century, daring young men and women with a

budding interest in gas-engine-powered machines found a variety of motorcycles available to them. From 1900 through 1903, small companies sprang up around Europe and North America offering their wares to riders everywhere.

"More Than 1,000 Riders"

In 1900, the Thomas Auto-Bi and the Orient became the first commercially produced motorcycles built in number in the United States. The Thomas Auto-Bi from the E. R. Thomas Motor Company of Buffalo, New York, and the Orient from the Waltham Manufacturing Company of Waltham, Massachusetts, set the style for most of the early American motorcycles to follow. Both the Auto-Bi and the Orient were essentially converted bicycles powered by single-cylinder gas engines fitted to modified diamond-shaped frames. Gas tanks were suspended from the main frame tubes or placed behind the rear seats, and power was carried to the rear wheels via leather belts. In fact, E. R. Thomas called his creation a "motor bicycle."

A 1902 advertisement described the Auto-Bi in an attempt to ease the fearful consumer's mind that motor bicycles were death machines: "The Thomas Auto-Bi entirely dissipates the popular conception that a motor bicycle is a heavy dangerous locomotive to be ridden only on the track by daredevils who invite death every time they mount the infernal machine." The purple prose continued to flow, describing the Auto-Bi with a refrain that could have described many of the motorcycles on the market by this time: "It is nothing but an ordinary bicycle made stronger to meet the new conditions."

Finding a market for motor bicycles was an uphill pull, however. In 1901, production of the Thomas Auto-Bi was taken over by the Buffalo Automobile & Auto-Bi Company. By 1902, the firm's ads proclaimed—rightly or wrongly—that "We are the largest manufacturers of Motor Cycles in the World. We have passed the experimental stage." There were now three versions of the Auto-Bi: the No. 3 with a 1½-hp engine; the No. 4 Racer and Roadster with a 2½-hp engine; and the deluxe No. 5, also with a 2½-hp engine, and costing a pretty penny for the time at $200. The ads went on to boast that there were "more than 1,000 riders" of the Auto-Bi.

"Get a Horse!"

The first motorcycles and automobiles—and perhaps the first aeroplanes, for all we know—were greeted with the angry suggestion, "Get a horse!" Looking back, the war cry seems quaint and prosaic, but at the time it was not merely a flat-earther's rant. Both horse owners and riders of the newfangled machines must have realized—or even feared—that they were standing at a turning point in history; some were charging forward with their throttle wide open, others were holding back—perhaps choking on the exhaust of the new machines, which was obviously the latest thing in manure as well.

It was only the beginning.

Thomas Auto-Bi Model No. 45 advertisement, 1907
Motorcycling was such a novel thrill that the Thomas Auto-Bi was advertised as being "Next to Flying," according to this early advertisement. Never fear—the Auto-Bi was designed from the start as a motorcycle (not an aeroplane) and was not a reconstituted bicycle, as the ad copy writers wanted you to be assured: "Every part of this machine is built for the exact purpose for which it is used. It's not a miscellaneous collection of parts placed on a bicycle."

Don't you know you can get the same sensations by tying firecrackers to your legs and sitting over an oil heater?
—Collier's *magazine, 1913*

1914 Wall Auto Wheel

Instead of bolting an engine into a bicycle's frame, as had become the convention, British engineer A. W. Wall went a different route, attaching it alongside on its own powered wheel. First offered in 1909, the Wall Auto Wheel was propelled by a 118-cc engine and could be added onto any bicycle, which was its major—and perhaps sole—advantage. It was also built under license by A. O. Smith & Company of Milwaukee, Wisconsin, as the Smith Auto Wheel starting in 1914. Top speed was a teeth-jarring 20 mph (32 kph). Owner: Carman Brown.

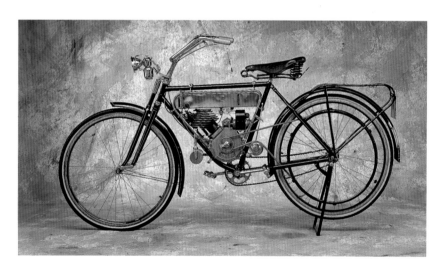

1908 CCM

Canada Cycle and Motor (CCM) of Weston, Ontario, was renowned for its bicycles in the late 1800s. In 1903, the firm's engineers were looking toward a brave new world when they unveiled their premier motorcycle. This new creation featured a 1½-hp, 241-cc single-cylinder engine sourced from the Swiss Motosacoche (MAG) firm and added to a CCM bicycle chassis. But Canadian roads were few and far between at the time, and the newfangled motorcycle was not a sales success, forcing CCM to quit motorcycle production circa 1912. Owner: Peter Gagan.

1910 EXCELSIOR AUTO-CYCLE MODEL KB30

Founded in 1908, the Excelsior Motor Manufacturing & Supply Company of Chicago, Illinois, was destined to become one of the great failed American motorcycle makers. This 1910 Model K was powered by a single-cylinder F-head engine of 30.50 ci (500 cc) that created 4 hp. In 1911, Chicago bicycle magnate Ignaz Schwinn bought Excelsior and catapulted the firm into competition with Indian and Harley-Davidson for prominence in the market. Alas, by 1931, Schwinn pulled the plug on Excelsior in the midst of the Great Depression, and the famous firm was no more. Owner: Reynolds-Alberta Museum.

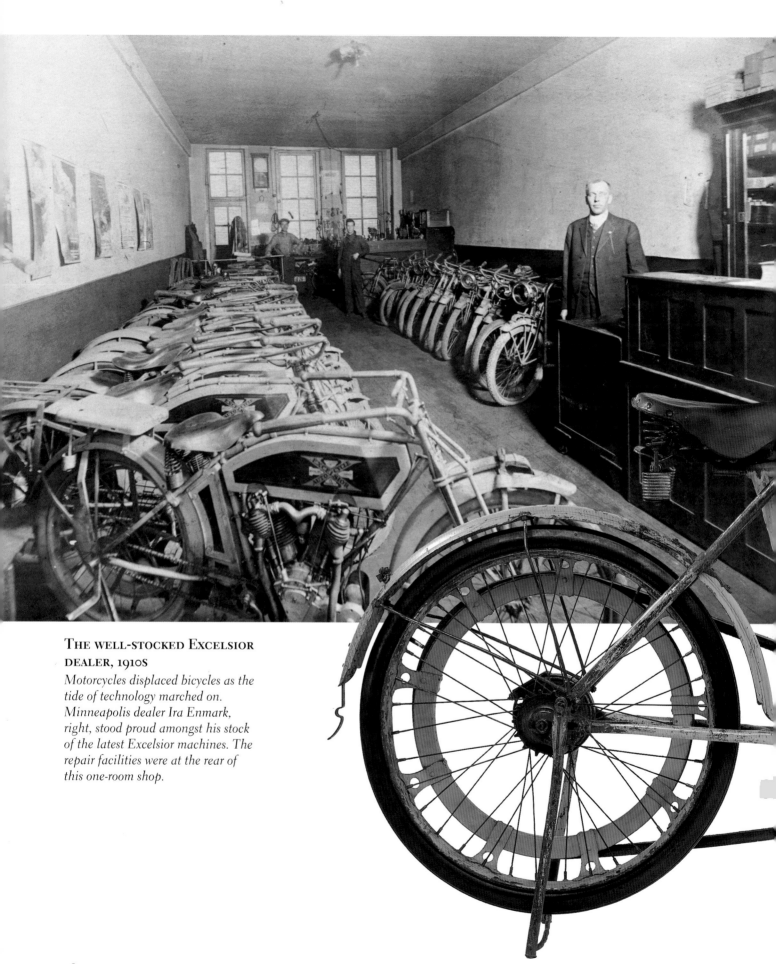

THE WELL-STOCKED EXCELSIOR
DEALER, 1910S

Motorcycles displaced bicycles as the tide of technology marched on. Minneapolis dealer Ira Enmark, right, stood proud amongst his stock of the latest Excelsior machines. The repair facilities were at the rear of this one-room shop.

1911 FLYING MERKEL

By the time this Flying Merkel was traveling down the road in 1911, the Merkel firm had evolved through three permutations—a common woe of the pioneering motorcycle enterprises. The Miami Cycle & Manufacturing Company of Middletown, Ohio, built this 61-ci (1,000-cc) V-twin, painted in Merkel's trademark garish orange. The Merkel featured a spring frame and fork, giving a ride that was heralded in ads as "the only motorcycle that doesn't shake the daylights out of its rider." By 1915, the great Merkel sadly was history. Owner: Reynolds-Alberta Museum.

Motor cyclists eat and sleep and talk like other folks, but at times they can't help feeling that they haven't as long to live as the ordinary man. And they are right. They are a fearless lot, brave enough to wear their lives on their sleeves, and have nerves as unimpressionable as flint.
—The New York Times, 1913

Chapter 2

KINGS OF THE ROAD

THE GLORY DAYS OF THE AMERICAN FOUR

HENRY FORD'S WORST NIGHTMARE, 1923

ABOVE: *Henry Ford feared sights such as this. In his worst dreams, he imagined families taking to motorcycles for everyday transportation like ducks to water, thus putting his Model T automobile out of business. This family and its fearless Fido were set for a spin on their Harley-Davidson sidecar unit in Bellevue, Alberta. (Photograph from Glenbow Archives)*

1930 HENDERSON KJ

LEFT: *In mid-1929, Henderson eschewed its old side-valve engines and unveiled a brand new F-head four-cylinder engine that it hoped would become the avant garde of the American motorcycling scene. Oddly enough, other makers were taking exactly the opposite route: Harley-Davidson was moving from F-heads to side-valves and Indian had offered an F-head Four since 1927. Still, the new Henderson KJ and its sibling KL sports model were glorious machines with sweeping streamlined styling that won plenty of converts. Owner: Ben Yarschenko.*

Henry Ford was afraid of motorcycles. The fear the father of the Model T automobile harbored for two-wheelers had nothing to do with actually having ridden or fallen off one of the infernal machines, however. Ford was afraid of what he saw as the sales potential for motorcycles.

Henry Ford had revolutionized the factory assembly process and given the world inexpensive mechanical transportation, putting people on four wheels with his sensational Model T of 1908 and doing the same for farmers with his radical lightweight Fordson tractor of 1916. Yet he saw a grave challenge to his kingdom in the form of the humble motorcycle. As he stated publicly in the mid-1910s, Ford feared that come the day when a lightweight motorcycle was produced at an inexpensive price, they would outsell his Ford cars—and spell doom for his empire.

In those heady days of the 1910s when anything seemed possible in the pioneering world of mechanical transportation, this fear appeared well founded to Ford. He himself was living proof of the potential of an inventive mind. Who knew what the future held?

THE GRAND DREAM

A young inventor named William G. Henderson shared a similar vision of the motorcycle's possibilities. Pioneering motorcycle visionaries before him had saddled bicycles with "infernal-combustion" engines to create crude single-cylinder motorcycles that could travel from point A to point B, but maybe not back again. Still others had grafted a second cylinder to the simple single and built the powerhouse V-twin. Will Henderson boasted a grander dream. He envisioned the ultimate machine, the pinnacle of motorcycles that all others would be compared to—a four-cylinder cycle.

The idea of a four-cylinder motorcycle was not new. The Belgian firm Fabrique Nationale (FN) had crafted the world's first four-cylinder cycle in 1908, and Pierce had built the first American four in 1910. But Will believed in himself and his mechanical abilities; he had faith that his four would be crowned the king of the road.

Will had the gifts of gumption and know-how to make his dream come true. Engineering ran in his blood. His famous grandfather, Alexander Winton, had sparked Winton Motor Carriage Company, builder of the respected Winton automobile. His father, Thomas Henderson, served as vice-president at Winton, and his elder brother, Thomas Jr., was a manager. Will also put in time learning the trade.

1930 HENDERSON KJ

Owner Ben Yarschenko: "My father often talked about going for rides on a big 1930 Henderson as a boy. Of course, what this did for me was bring about a mad hunt for one of these fabulous fours. I finally found one to restore. My not having ever heard a four run and my eagerness to do so brought about an accelerated restoration time involving long days and late nights. Even my neighbors looked forward to the engine's completion. So, when it finally came time to bring the engine to life, a small but intensely curious crowd joined me for the occasion—except that three o'clock in the morning maybe wasn't the best time to do it. What a sound!

"The big bike is easy to start after following a certain ritual common to many old bikes: With the bike on its side stand, I stand on the left side and give a mighty kick on the starter with my right foot, and there's that sound. I swing into the saddle, step on the foot clutch, pull the gearshift lever toward me for first gear, and with a little throttle, I ease off the clutch. It's an amazingly smooth ride, and there's lots of power. Top speed for this machine was originally claimed to be 105–110 mph, so normal highway speeds are easy to maintain.

"From some people I get nods of approval, but most people have never before heard of a Henderson motorcycle, and so they often get a little red in the face when they guess it's a modern bike and I tell them how old it is. My Henderson is a thrill to ride, and simply put, it gets all-out gawks from the public—just as a great old motorcycle should!"

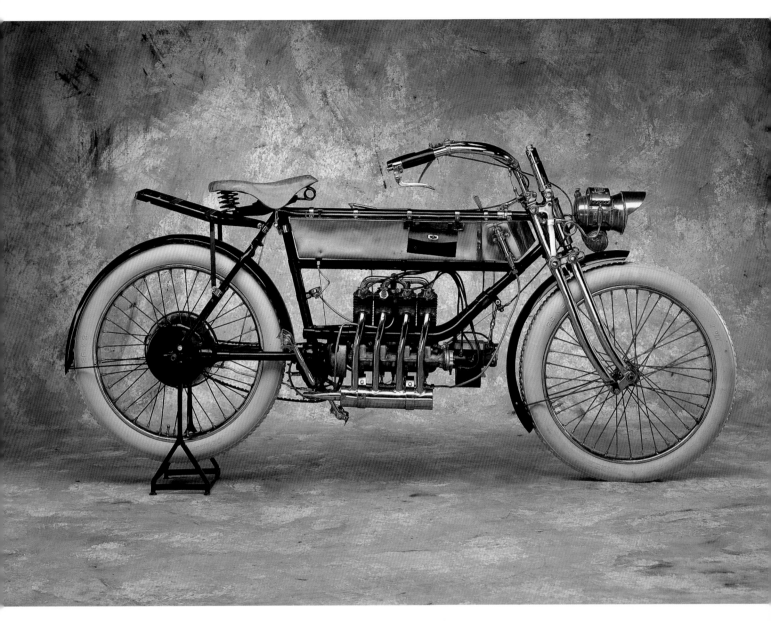

1910 FN

The Belgian Fabrique Nationale was famed for its armaments when it took the odd sidestep into building motorcycles in 1901. Following on the heels of the firm's first single came the astounding and audacious announcement that FN would unveil a four-cylinder in 1904 at a time when the rest of the world's fledgling motorcycle makers were still struggling to build reliable singles and the odd twin. Designed by farsighted engineer Paul Kelecom, FN's first four displaced 362 cc; this refined 1910 model featured a 410-cc engine with automatic inlet valves and shaft drive. It was truly an engineering marvel for its day. Owner: Peter Gagan.

A skittish motor-bike with a touch of blood in it is better than all the riding animals on earth, because of its logical extension of our faculties, and the hint, the provocation, to excess conferred by its honeyed untired smoothness.
—T. E. Lawrence, a.k.a. "Lawrence of Arabia"

1909 PIERCE

ABOVE: *In 1908, George Pierce of the great Pierce-Arrow Motor Car Company of Buffalo, New York, gave a gift to his only son, scion Percy Pierce. The present was his floundering Pierce bicycle-making firm, the venerable Pierce Cycle Company, and an old automobile factory. Percy immediately added an engine to one of the stodgy, old-fashioned bicycles and created a prototype motorcycle that evolved into the first Pierce single-cylinder of 1909. Percy soon bought himself an FN Four and, looking to the Belgian machine for "inspiration," created his own four in 1909. Percy's premier Fours featured a T-head engine similar to that of his father's cars, no clutch, and shaft drive. The Pierce Four was the first in a long line of great American fours, but the Pierce motorcycle firm lasted only until 1913. Owner: Eldon Brown.*

A SIGN OF THE TIMES, 1912

ABOVE: *Once a prominent bicycle maker, Pierce ads by the 1910s promoted the firm's single- and four-cylinder motorcycles, relegating mention of bicycle building to the small print.*

Yet the motorcycle, however many mechanical parts it may share with the automobile, was another beast altogether, and Will was drawn to two wheels instead of four. As with many budding young motorcyclists, however, his father stood in the way. In Will's case, though, his father presented a unique roadblock to his dreams—that of an experienced engineer. A motorcycle magazine of the day told Will's story based on an interview with his father:

"Ever since he was a boy he had an ambition to build motorcycles. I would try to discourage him, for I couldn't see any future for motorcycles then. I would point out defects in his plans and advise him to abandon the project, but a few weeks or months later he would be back again with sketches of a better design in which the objections I had pointed out were overcome. He was employed by a machine company in Cleveland at that time, but upon going home in the evening he would immerse himself in work on the design of a motorcycle, and stay at it until after midnight.

"Finally he came to me with a design worked out to the last detail. It was a full-size working drawing of a 4-cylinder motorcycle, complete down to every nut and bolt, with full specifications, in such a shape that a machine could be produced from those plans.

"I was afraid that he would make himself sick by overwork if he went on as he had been doing both day and night, so I had him give up his employment at the machine plant, and advanced money for constructing a model motorcycle of the design he had drawn up. I believed that when he encountered the practical difficulties incident to the building of an actual machine, he would be glad to drop it and should thus have it off his mind.

"But I was mistaken. With his attention freed of other duties he plunged into the work of building that motorcycle with all his energies. He worked night and day, hardly willing to stop to eat, and getting only a few scant hours of sleep."

Will drafted the designs for his first four-cylinder motorcycle in 1911. He was but twenty-nine years old.

Dash hither and yon in gay abandon.
—Salsbury Motor-Glide advertisement, 1936

THE ALLURE OF A FOUR

Will's motorcycle bore the family name, Henderson, on its elongated gas tank surmounting the simple word "Four." The word may have been simple, but the engineering was not.

While other manufacturers were struggling to build reliable single-cylinder machines, Will's creation was bold and audacious. The four cylinders were set inline, each boasting a bore and stroke measuring 2.50x3.00 inches (63.5x76 mm) for a displacement of 58.9 ci (982 cc). On this first prototype, drive to the rear wheel was via belt, as was typical on motorcycles of the time; subsequent production models would advance to chain drive. The engine was small in size but grand in stature, and its architecture was a model of mechanical efficiency with its single rear-mounted carburetor feeding the four cylinders through one long intake tract set above a stylish exhaust manifold.

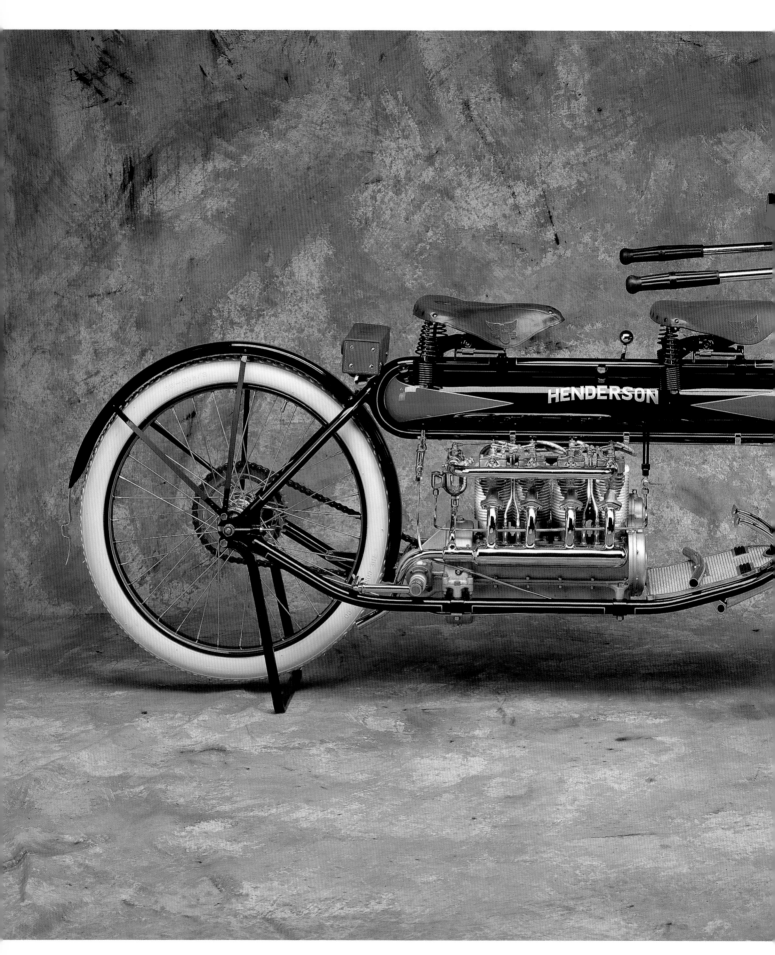

THE PERFECT GETAWAY MACHINE, 1915

ABOVE: *The advertiser's purple prose was much simpler in 1915.*

1912 HENDERSON MODEL A

LEFT: *Bill Henderson made stunning claims for his Model A four of 1912. He promoted the machine as making no noise nor vibration, statements that other motorcycle makers and riders must have chided—until they actually rode a Henderson, that is. The F-head engine displaced a magnificent 58.9 ci (965 cc), marking it as one of the largest and most powerful cycles of its day, which was all in keeping with Henderson's promotional braggadocio. With its passenger seat mounted in front of the driver, the four rode on a spacious 65-inch (162.5-cm) wheelbase. Comfort was king here, and floorboards were standard for the pilot and optional—mounted on the front forks—for the passenger. Owner: Carman Brown.*

1929 CLEVELAND TORNADO

Oddly enough, considering its later renown for its stunning fours, the Cleveland Motorcycle Manufacturing Company of Cleveland, Ohio, got its start building a two-stroke single—albeit probably the most successful two-stroke in American motorcycling history. The first Cleveland Four of 1926 was largely a copy of the Pierce Four, which in turn was a copy of the FN Four. Later in 1926, Cleveland launched a new Four, wholly designed by engineer Everett DeLong— although DeLong had formerly worked at Henderson and Ace. In 1929, Cleveland's Four evolved into the well-named Tornado, a flagship model with a refined T-head engine featuring futuristic magnesium pistons. But even with a top speed of 100 mph (161 kph), the Tornado was not able to outrun the effects of the Great Depression, and Cleveland ceased production in the same year its ultimate Four was unveiled. Owner: Eldon Brown.

Will's chassis also differed from those of many of the era's motorcycles. Most makers still relied on "diamond" bicycle frames; a handful of others were now using specially built "loop" frames. With different specifications required to fit a four, Will's frame was custom made for his engine and was an early example of a "cradle" frame— that is, with twin frame tubes wrapping around the engine, rather than having one lower tube extending underneath the sump. It was a style that would become the vogue for most motorcycles in the decades to follow.

Will's running prototype was a sight to behold in 1911, and after laying eyes on it, his brother, Tom Jr., was ready to follow where Will led. Together they started the Henderson Motorcycle Company of 268 Jefferson Avenue in Detroit, Michigan, with Tom as president due to his prowess as a manager and bookkeeper and Will as vice-president. Financial backing no doubt came from the Henderson and Winton families as well an infusion from others, including one odd source— W. E. Metsger, the Detroit dealer of the rival Indian motorcycle made by the Hendee Manufacturing Company of Springfield, Massachusetts, which by then was the largest motorcycle concern on the continent. The allure of a four-cylinder motorcycle was magical.

FORD BUYS A FOUR

Will and Tom Henderson started production of the Henderson Four as a 1912 model featuring several refinements over Will's 1911 proto-

type. The new Four was the most sophisticated machine on the road and must have made Model T owners green with envy and horseback riders have second thoughts about their oat-fueled transportation.

Will Henderson had little modesty when it came to describing the virtues of his creation. A 1912 advertisement for the Henderson Four bore the slogan "The Henderson—Ahead of Them All—It's the Most Modern in Motorcycle Construction." Above this statement ran a series of illustrations depicting the evolution of two-wheeled transport, from the days of the penny-farthing high-wheeler bicycle to the safety bicycle, on to the pioneering single-cylinder motorcycle—which was but the Missing Link—and then, finally, the ultimate evolution, the Henderson Four.

The Henderson won converts around the country, and one rider, Carl Stearns Clancy, was so enamored by the reliability of his Four that he set off in 1913 to accomplish the first tour around the world on a motorcycle. Another owner penned a testimonial proving the worth of four cylinders over a meager two: "On one occasion, about a month ago, I met a couple of fellows on the road with a 'twin' cylinder machine in trouble, I took them into Trenton at the end of a rope, a distance of 21 miles."

In fact, the Henderson was such a fine machine that one day in 1917, Tom Henderson answered his office telephone only to be surprised by the voice of none other than Henry Ford—"Hank" to his acquaintances like Henderson.

1924 ACE
Chaffing under the reigns of Ignaz Schwinn, Bill Henderson bucked his namesake firm and moved to Philadelphia, Pennsylvania, to establish the Ace Motorcycle Corporation. The debut Ace Four of 1920 bore a remarkable similarity to the Henderson Four, and it's a wonder that the cantankerous Schwinn didn't shut down the shop with a barrage of lawsuits. The Ace was powered by an inline F-head engine of 75 ci (1,229 cc) and weighed a hefty 395 pounds (178 kg). To add insult to Schwinn's economic injury, Henderson proudly proclaimed his new creation the "Perfected Four." Owner: Eldon Brown.

"Say, Tom, I want to buy a motorcycle," Ford said, to which Henderson replied, "I've always said you were a sensible man."

After hearing of a trans-continental record run by a Henderson, Ford sought one of the machines for his employees to use as a relay between his tractor factory and his farm, according to a Henderson ad of the day. Ford, ever the miser, naturally wanted a discount on the $370 retail price, but Henderson said no. Ford argued but Henderson stood firm. After more grumbling on Ford's part, an electrically equipped 1917 Henderson, paid for at full list price, was delivered that afternoon to Ford's tractor plant. Ever vigilant, Henry Ford was checking out the competition to put his worst fears to rest.

ENTER IGNAZ SCHWINN

Little did Henry Ford know, but there was another farsighted entrepreneur with two-wheeled designs on people's transportation dollars. A short, feisty German immigrant named Ignaz Schwinn had built a grand empire in Chicago by constructing bicycles. During the Gay Nineties, the newfangled bicycle had captured the world's attention, and the market exploded like nothing else before. As bicycle makers throughout North America cranked out their wares to the point of overproduction—and as the internal-combustion engine began to prove itself—the bicycle market crashed almost as dramatically as it had bloomed.

Schwinn, however, was one step ahead of the other bicycle makers. He had had a passion for engines from the first and built several automobiles of his own before deciding to leave the four-wheelers to Henry Ford; Schwinn believed motorcycles were the way of the future. His move seemed a reasonable step, marrying the technology of the two-wheeler that he had built his fortune upon with the modern wave of the gas engine that fueled his dreams.

Schwinn's engineers began drafting a shaft-driven vertical twin. When the new machine was ready to be built into a prototype, Schwinn suddenly switched directions. In 1911, he heard word that the Excelsior Motor Manufacturing & Supply Company was bankrupt. The Chicago firm had failed while building a fledgling motorcycle. On November 14, 1911, Schwinn anted up $500,000 and got a jump-start into the motorcycle business, quickly producing a line of Excelsior singles and twins. Schwinn's timing was perfect as motorcycles were just entering a boom market similar to that of the bicycle two decades before.

Then, opportunity struck

1928 INDIAN MODEL 401
Indian managers knew a good thing when they saw it: When the Ace firm came up for sale in 1927, Indian pounced. Moving stock to its Springfield empire, Indian relabeled and repainted Henderson's ultimate Four and began producing the new Indian Ace Four just months later. The first machines bore only the Ace name on the gas tank, but Indian was quick to add its image to the machines. By the time the Model 401 debuted, the gas tank moniker read "Indian 4" for all the world to see. Owner: Eldon Brown.

again just as Schwinn's design team was creating its own shaft-driven four-cylinder machine. Will and Tom Henderson's namesake motorcycle company was running into hard times due to World War I material shortages and the high price of their machine. Again, Schwinn stepped in, paid off the debts, hired the brothers, and transferred manufacture of the Henderson to his Excelsior plant. Now, Schwinn had a full line of machines, from his Excelsior singles and twins to the fine Henderson Four, which became the crown jewel of his line.

THE ACE FOUR

Will Henderson worked for Schwinn for just two years before he began to dream again of building his own four-cylinder motorcycle, over which he would have complete control. It was little surprise that he chafed under the yoke of Schwinn, given the maverick mindset that had inspired him to build a four in the first place.

While finishing the engineering plans for Schwinn's latest Henderson Model K, Will Henderson must have also been drafting ideas for his own new motorcycle as he was ready to start building his new machine just months after he left Schwinn in late 1919. Even with a non-compete contract from Schwinn hanging over his head, Henderson joined forces with Max Sladkin to found the Ace Motorcycle Corporation of Philadelphia, Pennsylvania.

The debut Ace Four of 1920 followed the form that Henderson had created for his earlier, namesake Fours. It was powered by an inline F-head engine of 75 ci (1,250 cc) and boasted styling that was rakish and streamlined. Ace's advertisements proudly labeled the machine the "Perfected Four," a sobriquet that must have been like a

1937 INDIAN SPORT FOUR MODEL 437

The name on the gas tank may have changed almost immediately, but it took years for the Ace Four to slowly but surely transform into the Indian Four. Indian redesigned the engine several times over the years—including its ill-fated "upside-down" Four of 1935 with exhaust valves set above the intake valves—and constantly refined the styling. The Indian Four grew increasingly more glamorous, but underneath it all, the lineage back to Bill Henderson's original Ace was always there. Owner: Carman Brown.

The greatest woman catcher I have ever seen.
—Air-racing ace Colonel Roscoe Turner on the
Salsbury Motor Glide scooter

1941 INDIAN FOUR MODEL 441
*Deeply valanced, "skirted" fenders appeared on the
Indian Four in 1940, creating a stylish ride beyond
anything available from Harley-Davidson. Over the years,
the Four's weight also grew from the Ace's lithe 455 pounds
(205 kg) up to a bloated 568 pounds (256 kg). Still, in
many enthusiasts' eyes, there never was a more beautiful
motorcycle than the ultimate Indian Four. During World
War II, Indian halted Four production to concentrate on
war materiel and never resumed it after the war years.
Owner: Trev Deeley Motorcycle Museum.*

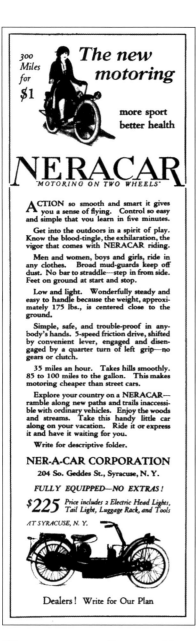

"BETTER HEALTH" WITH A NER-A-CAR, 1920S

As an interesting twist on the benefits of motorcycling, Ner-A-Car promoted "better health" in this advertisement: "Know the blood-tingle, the exhilaration, the vigor that comes with NERACAR riding."

knife in the side of Ignaz Schwinn.

In 1922, Ace hired the famous Erwin G. "Cannonball" Baker to publicize the firm's wares. Baker had set many a long-distance record on Indians, riding coast to coast in a halo of dust to add renown to the Iron Redskin's name. On September 22, 1922, Baker suited up in Los Angeles and jumped aboard his Ace Four with the goal of breaking an old Henderson Four transcontinental record. As he had once set a similar record on an Indian, Baker knew the unmarked route like the back of his hand and rode his Ace to the Atlantic in six days, twenty-two hours, and fifty-two minutes.

Flush with this success, Will Henderson laid plans for a new Ace Sport Solo Model, scheduled for 1923 production. On December 11, 1922, Henderson piloted the prototype onto the Philadelphia streets in the hopes of wringing out design flaws. Suddenly, an automobile dashed out of a side street and struck him down.

After Henderson's death, Sladkin struggled on with the Ace Four, but the heart of the company was gone. On January 27, 1927, all stock, patents rights, and "good will" of the Ace Motor Corporation were bought by Indian. The company's tools and inventory were moved to Springfield, and the Wigwam announced plans to start production of the new Indian Ace Four within thirty days.

DEATH KNELL FOR THE HENDERSON FOUR

At the Schwinn factory, the news of Indian's purchase of the Ace Four must have been greeted with a funereal silence. Competition for its flagship model from the one of the top two motorcycle makers was not welcome. By the dawn of the Great Depression in 1929, the end of the Henderson Four was looming. The Four cost a cool $435—about the same as one of Henry Ford's Model A automobiles.

Then, a blow struck closer to Ignaz Schwinn's heart when the star of the Excelsior race team, Bob Perry, was killed during a board-track race. Perry had been like a son to Schwinn, and his death hit hard.

With Perry's demise and the Great Depression worsening, Schwinn decided to call it quits. The General Motors Corporation of Pontiac, Michigan, had approached him about buying his motorcycle company, but with the economic downturn, the big carmaker lost interest. In 1931, Schwinn called a meeting of his employees and announced simply, "Gentlemen, today we stop." With those few, unsentimental words, Ignaz Schwinn retired, and the Excelsior and Henderson motorcycle lines were laid to rest.

Henry Ford felt the effects of the Great Depression as well, but his Model A juggernaut was already on a roll. Folks had come to not only rely on Ford's automobiles, they now prized them. People realized that automobiles were inexpensive to buy and economical to operate; they provided a modicum of reliability and gave shelter from the weather while on the road. Ford had won the war. Following World War I, the motorcycle in North America would largely be a hobbyist's toy or a sport plaything, while automobiles came to rule the roads.

It was nearly a car and nearly a motorcycle, but in the end it was not enough of either.

The Ner-A-Car was the brainchild of Carl Neracher. Unable to gain backing for his creation, Neracher inspired Sheffield Simplex, Ltd. of England in starting Ner-A-Car production in 1920. With success in England, financing was found in the United States and the Ner-A-Car Corporation of Syracuse, New York, began building machines in 1921. Production was also licensed in Canada.

The Ner-A-Car bristled with innovative ideas. It was powered by a 211-cc, two-stroke, single-cylinder engine, a rare use of two-stroke technology in an early American machine. The engine and gearbox were enclosed in a monocoque belly that served as a unitized frame. Footboards and a skirted front fender provided protection from road spray. Instead of the usual front fork, the front wheel was turned by a pioneering form of hub-center steering.

Alas, folks didn't cotton to the Ner-A-Car: Those that wanted a car, bought a car. Ner-A-Car production ground to a halt in 1924, although the Sheffield Simplex remained in production in England until 1926.

BATHING BEAUTIES AND NER-A-CAR FLEET, 1920S
A bevy of bathing beauties displayed the graces of the Ner-A-Car. (Photograph from Frank Westfall/Syracuse Ner-A-Car Museum)

1922 NER-A-CAR

OWNER **CLIFF ZIMMERMAN:** "I bought my 1922 Ner-A-Car in 1988 at an auction sale in Milton, Ontario. After transporting it home, I was anxious to start it. First, I hooked up the spark plug. Then I mixed a 20:1 two-stroke gas mixture and poured it into the tank. Surprise, no leaks!

"Opening the gas petcock was the next step. Which way was on? This way or that way? I wondered what kind of carb does the engine have? Better yet, where is it? I peered below and found it hiding under the front mudguard, up by the steering column. Looking down through a hole where the steering column passes through the mudguard, I could see a tickler on top of the carb. With the rubber tip of a pencil, I pressed the tickler and held it down. Momentarily, gas gushed out of a hole in the middle of the tickler. Ah ha! The petcock must be open! My heartbeat quickened. Will this beast actually start?

"The two throttle control levers are on the handlebar. I thought, why two levers? I moved them about one quarter from idle. Standing on the left side of the machine, I forced the kickstart lever downward. The compression could be felt midway through the lever's travel. There was fuel, air, compression, and rotation: All the components of ignition were present. Now it was judgment time! I shoved the kickstart lever rapidly from top to bottom. It started with just one goddamn kick!

"The engine roared to life and smoke billowed from under the machine. It made a hit-and-miss sound: Putt pa pa pa putt pa pa putt. I let it putt and smoke and shake until it was warmed up. I plunked myself down onto the saddle. Twisting the left-handed clutch grip, the friction-drive transmission engaged, and the machine lurched into motion. I was off! The ride was surprisingly smooth, and I felt I was indeed on the Rolls-Royce of scooters. My heart swelled. I was in love again. I rode along the street I live on. When a mother and her young daughter caught sight of the Ner-A-Car, the child let out a gleeful shriek but was totally at a loss for words. No explanation came from her mother. As time and my Ner-A-Car rolled on, this reaction came to be typical, even from Harley and Indian riders. They would stop their machines, marvel and wonder, and even give me wanton and envious looks."

A little less prejudice and a wider recognition of the reliability of the motorcycle will be a means of extending to more people a very exhilarating recreation as well as an economical means of transportation, which is unfortunately considered by many to be beneath them.
—The New York Times, 1912

1922 NER-A-CAR

The Ner-A-Car moniker not only described the automotive leanings of the machine but was also a pun on the name of its designer, Carl Neracher. Owner: Clifford Zimmerman.

Chapter 3

THE
CYCLONE

THE NEED FOR SPEED

MOTORDROME ACTION, 1913

ABOVE: *Motorcycles circle the 58-degree banking at the Milwaukee Motordrome. As with most motordromes throughout the United States, the track was made of pine boards. When the boards were freshly laid, riders suffered burst tires from wood splinters—splinters that were reported to at times be up to a foot (30 cm) long and could also lance riders themselves.*

CYCLONE RACER

LEFT: *The Cyclone was a dream come true. Designed by Swedish immigrant Andrew Strand and built by Fred Joerns's Joerns-Thiem Motor Manufacturing Company of St. Paul, Minnesota, the Cyclone was created for one purpose only: to rule the board-track motordromes. The name "Cyclone" should have been a warning to other riders and builders, conjuring up the image of a whirling wind around the circular saucer tracks. The Cyclone made its debut on June 21, 1914, at the Twin City Motordrome in St. Paul, where rider J. A. "Demon" McNeil not only won the first race the Cyclone entered, but also shattered the track's three-mile (4.8-km) record en route. (Photograph © Stephen Wright)*

With eloquence fueled by fire and brimstone, the preachers were warning their flocks. From the pulpits of their churches, the preachers cast stones against their neighbor, the brand-spanking-new Twin City Motordrome that had been built at the intersection of Hamline and University Avenues, midway between Minneapolis and St. Paul, Minnesota. Workers had broken ground in May 1914 and started erecting the pine-board saucer track under the direction of owner Harry T. Koeln, who spent $50,000 to build the motordrome, according to local newspapers. The clergymen were enraged by the coming of this latest sign of modern-day decadence.

The St. Paul newspaper reported that one reverend railed to the state public safety commissioner: "While my church is more than a mile from the Motordrome, the noise of the machines could be heard distinctly during the services a week ago Sunday." Another pastor denounced the noise as "unbearable."

Motorcycle racing fans felt otherwise.

Motordromes were all the rage around the country. On a Saturday night in 1914, you had your choice of seeing Buffalo Bill's Wild West Show, a live re-enactment of the Bible at a local vaudeville house, or perhaps a baseball game down at the ballpark. Or you could see a motorcycle race, which was the most dramatic, *modern* event available. As the Minneapolis *Journal* enthused about the new motordrome in a fine flow of the best purple prose of the day: "East and west the motordrome is the star show place. No one in California cities that sport motordromes would think of going any place else for a fine evening sport. No more in the east. Motordroming gets into the blood. Moving things take the public fancy these days and at motordromes things do move. That's what people pay for: to see the motorcycles go round at frightful speed."

In the 1910s, motorcycles were the pinnacle of technology, achieving speeds that were hard to fathom in the days when *fast* meant riding a horse or, at best, an iron horse. To citizens fascinated by new developments in the newfangled gas-powered internal-combustion engine, a motorcycle was the ultimate machine, and the excitement of

"Speed: The Twentieth Century Sport," 1914

"A Thrill Every Minute" promised this poster for the newly opened Twin City Motordrome, where fans could see what was "By far the most fascinating sport ever introduced."

SPEED SPEED

TWIN CITY MOTORDROME
THE TWENTIETH CENTURY SPORT

Midway Between Minneapolis and St. Paul—University and Snelling Avenues
One Fare From Either City—Take Any Interurban ("St. Paul-Minneapolis") Street Car

NOW OPEN

Races Tonight

And Every Wednesday, Saturday and Sunday Night
BEGINNING AT 8:30 P. M.

See the Fastest Motorcycle Riders in the World in Action on America's Fastest Board Track

A THRILL EVERY MINUTE

Seven Fast Contests on Each Program, the Contestants competing for Liberal Cash Prizes. They Travel Faster Than NINETY MILES AN HOUR.

BY FAR THE MOST FASCINATING SPORT EVER INTRODUCED.

BAND CONCERTS AND OTHER ENTERTAINING FEATURES ARE A PART OF EACH MEETING. A GOOD WAY TO ENJOY THE HOT SUMMER EVENINGS.

Always—POPULAR PRICES—Always

Automobiles Admitted to the Paddock Free of Charge.   EVERY SEAT A GOOD ONE.

1908 INDIAN V-TWIN RACER

From the dawn of the 1900s until 1908 when this racer was built, Indian ruled the roost in North American motorcycling racing. Indian first created a V-twin for competition in 1906; V-twin cycles for the road did not appear in the catalog until 1907. This V-twin racer's 38.6-ci (633-cc) F-head engine fathered 4–5 hp, almost double the power of an Indian single. The chain-driven speedometer attached to the rigid front fork; it read up to 80 mph (128 kph) although top speed was 75 mph (129 kph). Owner: David Banks.

EXCELSIOR TEAM, 1913

ABOVE: A proud team of Canadian riders encircle the Excelsior V-twin that carried them to numerous victories. Throughout the 1910s, Excelsior's F-head racers warred with Indian's overhead-valve V-twins, which boasted four valves per cylinder. In December 1912, an Excelsior V-twin was the first motorcycle to break 100 mph (161 kph) at a sanctioned record-setting event. It was a trophy that Indian sorely wished was its own. (Photograph from Provincial Archives of Alberta)

RACE WINNER, 1913

LEFT: An exhausted-looking winner of the Edmonton Fair race in Canada rested aboard his Excelsior V-twin. (Photograph from Provincial Archives of Alberta)

speed was a novel thrill. American poet Walt Whitman had sung the body electric in the heady days of electricity's discovery; now there was a philosophical movement called Modernism that, like most such movements, stood for throwing out the old and embracing all that was new. Modernism's chief philosopher, Italian artiste Fillippo Tommaso Marinetti, swooned over the concept of pure speed: "We say that the world's magnificence has been enriched by a new beauty: the beauty of speed. A racing car whose hood is adorned with great pipes, like serpents of explosive breath—a roaring car that seems to ride on grapeshot—is more beautiful than the Victory of Samothrace . . . . Time and Space died yesterday. We already live in the absolute, because we have created eternal, omnipresent speed."

Yet, motordromes offered still another thrill to the people who crowded the stands—blood. Board-track races were like Roman chariot races of yore. A burst tire at full speed could send a motorcycle pilot careening across the track, and stories of horrific crashes at other motordromes were part of the pull to the crowd.

It was the noise, spectacle of speed, and sheer bloodthirstiness of motordrome racing that had whipped the local preachers into a frenzy usually reserved for visions of the coming of the Antichrist. Little did the preachers—or most motorcycle fans, for that matter—know but such a coming was about to break its way into the motorcycle world at the Twin City Motordrome with the arrival of a new motorcycle, the Cyclone.

THE SAUCER TRACKS

The first motorcycle race likely took place when two motorcyclists met for the first time and naturally had to see whose mechanical stallion was the quicker. Organized races in the early days were often held on country roads closed off for the event. Because paved roads were rare at the dawn of motorcycling, racing naturally grew up on dirt. Soon, races were held at county and state fairs on the dirt tracks usually reserved for horse racing.

Since motorcycles were developed as mechanized pacing machines for bicycle racing at velodromes, it was only natural that motorcycles were pitted against each other on these banked bicycle venues, perhaps as an intermission between the pedal-powered races. But new was better, and the motorcycles soon usurped the fans' applause.

The first motordrome was built in 1909 in Clifton, New Jersey. Construction of the Clifton motordrome followed the style of local velodromes and boasted 25-degree banked corners. Motordromes were typically built at the end of street-car lines on inexpensive land at the edge of a city. Street-car companies helped promote the tracks as they gave riders a destination at the end of their lines, as were amusement parks, with which motordromes often shared space.

Other motordromes also opened in 1909, including the Los Angeles Coliseum in Los Angeles, California, and the Springfield, Massachusetts, motordrome in Indian's hometown. To the thrill of the

Never had he sensed such gigantic power under him, and he felt exalted to the skies. He forgot everything in the mad delirium of speed; tremendous, maddening speed.
—J. W. Duffield, *Bert Wilson's Twin Cylinder Racer*, 1914

crowd, local riders mounted atop their Indian, Merkel, Thor, Reading Standard, and Excelsior cycles burned round the tracks.

Motordromes were an instant hit, so more saucer tracks were erected. In 1910, three new board tracks were opened: the one-mile Playa del Rey in Venice, California; the Wandemere Motordrome in Salt Lake City, Utah; and the Tuleries in Denver, Colorado. In 1911, the half-mile Elmhurst Motordrome in Oakland, California, and the Riverview Motordrome in Chicago, Illinois, started business. Los Angeles Stadium and Brighton Beach Motordrome on Coney Island, New York, began hosting races in 1912. Over the next four years, more opened in Detroit, Michigan; Newark, New Jersey; Point Breeze in Philadelphia, Pennsylvania; St. Louis, Missouri; Cleveland, Ohio; and Omaha, Nebraska. Motordrome riders began touring the United States seeking big purses at the venues. An official league was formed, and the sport continued to draw record numbers of fans.

Then, on the penultimate day of 1912, rider Lee Humiston broke the 100-mph (161-kph) mark at the Playa de Rey, California, motordrome on a 61-ci (1,000-cc) big-valve open-port V-twin Excelsior. The war for speed at the motordromes and for technical excellence within the factory race shops had intensified to a point years ahead of the similar wars in aviation and automobile design.

Racing on board tracks was an anomaly in the history of motorcycling, although one of the most exciting and bloodthirsty kind. Motordrome racing came and went in eight short years—1909 through 1916—but to many, it remains the pinnacle of the sport, an almost unbelievable, near-mythical style of racing.

1949 HARLEY-DAVIDSON WR
Harley-Davidson's WR was one of the legendary American racing motorcycles, with mountains of trophies and miles of race victories to its credit. The model was launched in 1941 to combat Indian's reigning Sport Scout, and it soon became a favorite of privateer racers everywhere in "showroom stock" Class C events. The WR's iron-barreled, side-valve, 45-ci (737-cc) V-twin engine was almost bulletproof, and the three-speed gearbox was all that was needed for dirt-tracking. Amazingly, the WR still won races for years after it went out of production. Owner: Trev Deeley Motorcycle Museum.

A NEW AGE OF TECHNOLOGY

Despite the dire warnings of the preachers, opening night at the Twin City Motordrome on May 30, 1914, was a sight to behold. Some 18,000 eager fans crowded the stands as $1,000 worth of fireworks were set alight, heralding a new age of technology in the Twin Cities. Everyone who was anyone was there. Minnesota Governor A. O. Eberhart arrived in state with his military escort and orated on patriotic themes. The St. Paul mayor waved to the crowd as a brass band played and vaudeville acts performed.

The quarter-mile Twin City track followed the style set by the other popular board tracks around the country, which were built primarily by motordrome impresario Jack Prince, who had made the new sport a raging success. The Twin City racetrack was a pure circle banked all of the way around at the astounding angle of 58 degrees.

The surface of the track was made of pine boards. While it was new, riders would suffer burst tires from wood splinters—splinters that were reported to be up to a foot long and could lance riders as well.

The boards would eventually become soaked in the oil spit out by the engines and lose their roughness as the motorcycles lapped the saucer track.

Around the outside of the Twin City track were nine rows of bench seats that could hold 10,000 fans; there was standing room for another 6,000. Inside the track was a large central area that served as a paddock for race teams as well as a drive-in area for other fans who could watch the goings-on from the comfort of their Model T Fords. The entire motordrome was full on opening night, with huge lights towering above the track lending a carnival atmosphere to the events. As soon as the last speech had echoed away over the motordrome and the brass band quieted their instruments, the first of five races began.

As riders straddled their mounts, their pit crews pushed them off, and they dropped in their clutches to start their engines. The pilots circled their Indians and Excelsiors around the flat base of the banking until they were up to speed, then angled up the saucer. After a couple warm-up laps, the riders rolled into unison, and a newfangled electric starting wire let the race begin.

Probably the best—or at least most colorful—eyewitness description from the times was penned by J. W. Duffield in his popular novel of 1914 entitled *Bert Wilson's Twin Cylinder Racer*, describing Bert Wilson's ride aboard his "Blue Streak" motorcycle:

"The whole machine quivered and shook under the mighty impact of the pistons, and the hum of the flywheels rose to a high

MUSTANG SPEED RUN, 1952
Mustang salesman-turned-racer Walt Fulton topped 100 mph (161 kph) on a souped-up Mustang hot rod at Rosamond dry lake in California. Fulton's flat-out style was designed to cut wind drag, a pose that Rollie Free also used on a Vincent Black Lightning, which he rode in only a bathing suit to beat Harley-Davidson's speed record. But Fulton eschewed the big motorcycles as competition for the Mustang: "I could have been riding it hands off at 100 mph."

1961 Matchless G50

ABOVE: *Matchless's 496-cc G50 was a grown up version of the 350-cc AJS 7R "Boy Racer." Launched in 1958, the G50 challenged Harleys and Indians on North American racetracks throughout the 1960s, continuing to take the checkered flag even after its brief production run ended in 1962. Fifty G50 CSR street models were also built in 1961 to homologate the G50 for competition. Both the G50 and CSR versions boasted 46.5 hp on tap from the single-cylinder "thumper" engine. Owner: Scona Cycle and Sports.*

1959 Norton Manx 40M

LEFT: *Norton's Manx is without doubt one of the most famous racing motorcycles of all time. It also may have borne the brunt of more curses than any other, especially from American riders whose Harleys and Indians finished second behind Manxes when the Nortons first invaded U.S. races. Launched in 1946 in both the 348-cc 40M Junior and 498-cc 30M Senior versions, the Manx was the first "foreign" motorcycle many North American riders had to contend with—and often, lose to. Owner: Murray Neibel.*

When you race cycles, you take spills, 'cause you're out there twisting the tiger's tail.
—Steve McQueen

BROADSLIDE, 1960S

*A Harley-Davidson pilot broadslided
his machine through a turn on the
horse-racing track during Minnesota
State Fair festivities.*

whine. Violet flames shot from the exhaust in an endless stream.

"The track streamed back from the whirling wheels like a rushing river. It seemed to be leaping eagerly to meet him. The lights and shadows flickered away from him, and the grotesque shadow cast by his machine weaved rapidly back and forth as he passed under the sizzling arc lights.

"The spectators were a yelling mob of temporary maniacs by this time. The Frenchman and Englishman had passed the eighty-mile mark, and Bert was still a lap and a half behind. He was riding like a fiend, coaxing, nursing his machine, manipulating the controls so as to wring the last ounce of energy from the tortured mass of metal he bestrode. . . .

"Suddenly, without any warning, something—nobody ever learned what—went wrong. They became a confused, tangled mass of blazing machine and crumpled humanity. Bert was not twenty feet behind them, and men turned white and sick and women fainted. It seemed inevitable that he would plow into them traveling at that terrific pace, and add one more life to the toll of the disaster.

"Bert's mind acted like a flash. He was far down on the track, and could not possibly gain a position above the wreckage, and so skirt it in that way. Nor did he have time to pass beneath it, for men and machines were sliding diagonally down the steep embankment.

"With a muttered prayer, he accepted the last chance fate had seen fit to leave him. He shot off the track completely, and whirled his machine onto the turf skirting it.

"The grass was smooth, but, at Bert's tremendous speed, small obstacles seemed like mountains. The 'Blue Streak' quivered and bounded, at times leaping clear off the ground, as it struck some uneven place. For what seemed an age, but was in reality only a few seconds, Bert kept on this, and then steered for the track again. If his machine mounted the little ridge formed by the beginning of the track proper, all might yet be well, if not—well, he refused to even think of that.

"The front wheel hit the obstruction, and, a fraction of a second later, the rear wheel struck. The machine leaped clear into the air, sideways. Bert stiffened the muscles of his wrists until they were as hard as steel, to withstand the shock of landing. The handlebars were almost wrenched from his control, but not quite, and once more he was tearing around with scarcely diminished speed. . . .

"Bert was now less than half a lap behind the flying leaders, but he had only four miles in which to make it up. At intervals now he leaned down and pumped extra oil into the engine. This added a trifle of extra power, and as he rushed madly along the 'Blue Streak' lived up to its name nobly. At the beginning of the last mile he was only about three lengths behind. The vast crowd was on its feet now, shouting, yelling, tossing hats, gesticulating. They were worked up to a pitch of frenzy absolutely indescribable.

"As Bert crept grimly up, nearer and nearer, the place became a veritable Bedlam. Now the racers had entered the last lap; only a third

1966 Jawa-ESO speedway racer

While the Czech firm Jawa built a vast array of motorcycles from its debut model of 1929, the make is best remembered for its stark and purposeful speedway racers. The glory was largely inherited, however: Jawa took control of fellow Czech firm ESO in 1966, gaining ESO's speedway cycles and motocrossers. This racer was powered by a 497-cc single pumping out 50 hp at 8,000 rpm. Weight was a sprightly 182 pounds (83 kg). Owner: Zoli Berenyi Sr.

1968 Norton-Curtis

It's an ironic rule of motorcycling lore that the better loved a model is, the more special versions and aftermarket customizing surrounds the machine. Norton's Commando was a perfect case in point. Norton offered numerous variations on the basic Commando model, including the Production Racer version, John Player Norton race replica, and more. The aftermarket also jumped merrily aboard the Commando, with Dunstall and others offering a range of performance accessories. This road-race Commando was built for 750-cc superbike road racing at Daytona. The Seeley Mk II–patterned frame was built in Vancouver, British Columbia, by Dennis Curtis using Reynolds 531 tubing. The engine was a modified Commando unit with Dunstall alloy barrels, Carrillo rods, Axtel Daytona cams, and a Quaiffe five-speed gearbox. The cycle weighed a mere 300 pounds (135 kg). Owner: Peter Gagan.

of a mile to go, and Bert was still a length behind. The exhaust of the racing motorcycles united in one hoarse, bellowing roar, that seemed to shake the very earth.

"Then Bert reached down, and with the finish line but a short hundred yards ahead, opened wide the air shutter on the carburetor. His machine seemed to almost leave the track, and then, tearing forward, passed the Frenchman, who was leading. As he crossed the finish line, Bert was ahead by the length of a wheel!"

As the headlines of the Twin Cities' newspapers shouted the day after the first races: "Thrills In Plenty At Motordrome."

THE CYCLONE

In the preachers' minds, it all spelled trouble. Over the next month of racing, there were crashes, spills, and motorcycles starting afire at speed—all of which drew more crowds. This was bad enough, but even in the preachers' worst visions they could not have guessed at what was coming next.

On the night of Saturday, June 21, 1914, rider Jock "Demon" McNeil of Salt Lake City, Utah, a Twin City Motordrome regular, rolled a new mount out under the board track's lights. Scotsman McNeil had raced a homemade, overhead-valve JAP-engined special in 1912 before switching to an Excelsior. But this new machine was something special. Painted in a brilliant, audacious yellow, it was not the product of one of the established eastern factories, but was rather a home-brewed, locally made upstart, a challenger to the board-track throne. Across the tank, in curlicued letters was the logo "Cyclone," with the name of the manufacturer written in smaller type on the elongated tail of the fanciful first "C": "Joerns Motor Mfg. Co. St. Paul, Minn."

The June 21, 1914, edition of the Minneapolis *Journal* had promised that "Spectators at races at the Twin City motordrome are soon to see J. A. McNeil, one of the fast boys now competing there, on a new mount, according to a report from the Midway course last night. McNeil it was learned, has been trying out a new Thiem racing contrivance with a marked degree of success. The motorcycle was made at the factory of the Joerns Thiem company in Midway. No official time of the trial was made, but it was declared a high average was piled up. Reports were heard that the rider has been made an offer to ride a Thiem the remainder of the season."

The other teams with their established Indian and Excelsior mounts must have laughed at the chances of such a new, homegrown machine. Any laughter would quickly come to an end.

St. Paul and Minneapolis had long been a center of motorcycle manufacturing, even though the history of the motorcycle itself was young. Among the first firms was Edward A. Thiem's Thiem Manufacturing Company of St. Paul, which had been "building motors and complete motorcycles for the jobbing trade and large dealers who have been advertising and selling these machines under their own names and as their own make," as *Motorcycle Illustrated* reported on April 20, 1911.

AT SPEED, 1960S

Dirt-tracker Jay Springsteen takes to the tarmac on a Harley-Davidson XRTT, the road-race version of the famed XR750 dirt-track specialist. Springsteen was quite possibly the most popular Harley-Davidson rider in recent time, a sort of down-home super hero that kept the orange-and-black flag flying during the firm's dark days.

1974 Yamaha TZ700

Yamaha was a musical instrument manufacturer that decided to take the odd step of diversifying into motorcycles. In 1954, it released a copy of the German DKW RT125; it began shipping subsequent models to the United States in 1960. But it was Yamaha's TZ700 that won the Japanese firm respect. After the water-cooled TZ Series replaced the previous air-cooled TDs in 1973, a TZ250 or TZ350 twin or a TZ700/ TZ750 four was a requisite for privateer racers who harbored any hope of success. The big TZs dominated Formula 750 racing throughout the 1970s, winning four championship titles and still sweeping the Daytona 200 as late as 1982. Owner: Dave Franklyn.

1974 Yamaha TZ700

Owner Dave Franklyn: "Having raced TZ250 and 350 bikes, I was expecting a similar type of powerband on the TZ700, but my first few laps at the track revealed it was definitely a different breed. This engine had incredible torque under 6,000 rpm. Above that, its acceleration was breathtaking.

"I had never been one who liked feeling overwhelmed by a bike's power, so I needed to learn how to control it, while also trying to control my nerves. Speed can be tough on the nerves, but matching speed to a track presents the ultimate anxiety for a guy on a new bike. My first few experiences at the track gave me the sensation of being picked up as I came out of one corner and then thrown at unbelievable speed to the next corner. I would always feel like I arrived there much too suddenly. Then, trying not to panic, I would have to shift down through the gears to cut my speed before taking the curve. Sometimes, being pushed to the limits could be a great thrill, but there were other times when my brain could hardly keep up to the pace.

"I soon learned not to use the back brake as this bike only weighs about 320 pounds, so it would tend to come off the ground with too much braking. Instead, I'd keep just two fingers on the front brake lever and only give it a gentle squeeze when really necessary. If I made the front brake bite too hard, I would either be thrust up onto the tank, or I'd have to use all my strength to keep from being sent right over the front. I gradually got to know and appreciate the bike's tricky braking, its fierce acceleration, its flexing frame, its narrow tires, and its top speed of 180 mph. By then I had decided that maybe only those with ample hair on their chests could handle such intimidation.

"The TZ700 astonished the motorcycle world when it was introduced. Yamaha only produced 200 of them during '74 and '75, yet the demand was so great that a resume was required to get one. I wasn't surprised when I heard that some enthusiasts offered to pay double the price.

"I'll never forget how I felt after my first race on this bike. I stood there staring at it—I was a total wreck—and there it stood, staring back at me, composed, silent, and ready for its next victim."

1989 HONDA RC30

Honda's VFR750R "RC30" was a hand-built, limited-edition replica of the factory RVF racebike. The RVF dominated endurance racing and Formula One events in the mid-1980s, and Honda fans quickly bought out the run of RC30 replicas. Propelled by a 112-hp version of the VFR750 engine, the lightweight and compact RC30 was a superb ride. Owner: Jeff Bauer.

Launching a fledgling motorcycle was an uphill battle, however, and in 1911, Thiem joined forces with the young black sheep scion of a prominent St. Paul furniture-building family, Fred Joerns. The Joerns family ran a flagship furniture store in the city and oversaw three factories in different states. Fred Joerns had little love for furniture but was fascinated by the technology of the pioneering automobiles and motorcycles, and so stepped in to run the newly named Joerns-Thiem Motor Manufacturing Company.

Among the debts and unfinished projects that Joerns inherited was a new motorcycle engine design created by factory superintendent Andrew Strand. Strand was a recent immigrant from Sweden and a confirmed tinkerer. Minneapolis was one of the largest flour-milling centers in the world at the time, and so it was little surprise that the Twin Cities were also home to numerous early farm tractor and agricultural implement makers, which likely interested Strand as he later designed and built a governor for Henry Ford's revolutionary Fordson tractor.

In 1912, Joerns-Thiem launched its own single-cylinder Thiem motorcycle powered by an early side-valve engine. The side-valve was an engine design pioneered in the United States by Reading-Standard in 1906 that did not win widespread acceptance until Indian converted to side-valves with its Powerplus of 1916 and Harley-Davidson took to side-valves in 1929.

Strand's new engine design, however, was decades ahead of its time. The layout of the engine followed the established American V-twin as used by Indian, Excelsior, Harley-Davidson, and others, but the revolution came in Strand's overhead-camshaft drive. Overhead cams were not new: The setup had been used previously on a French Peugeot race car, among others. But overhead cams were novel on motorcycles, and the engineering needed to make the system work was intricate and pioneering. Strand created a masterpiece.

The engine's overhead cams were run through a series of beautifully machined bevel gears. A bevel gear on the end of the engine pinion shaft drove shafts running vertically up the right sides of the two cylinders to drive the overhead camshafts via another set of bevel gears. Running off a bevel gear drive on the front cylinder shaft was a shorter shaft that drove the magneto.

The overhead valve gear was also unique to the Cyclone, with rockers pulling the valves down to open them, rather than pushing them open as on other cycles. This setup cut valve guide wear, a common weak point on engines of the day.

The 61-ci (1,000-cc) engine with its ported cylinders was mounted in a typical rigid racing frame with chain drive to the rear wheel. Brakes were eschewed, as they were considered too dangerous, which was a distinct possibility considering the quality of brakes of the day and the speeds achieved on boardtracks.

When the first Cyclone was built is difficult to pinpoint. Cyclone historian Bob Chantland believes the premier prototype may have been built as early as 1912; historian Jerry Hatfield states that the Cyclone debuted as a 1913 model. Prototypes were undoubtedly built before the motorcycle's reported debut at the motordrome as it ran without reported trouble or breakdowns and finished or won its races. The first notice in the Twin Cities newspapers of the Cyclone appears in connection with the motordrome and Cyclone tests on June 20, 1914. The newspaper reporters covering the motordrome were not especially knowledgeable motorcycling enthusiasts, judging by the general, vague tone of their writing, and it's possible they did not hear of earlier tests. Because the Joerns-Thiem works was located within blocks of the motordrome, however, it seems likely that the Cyclone was developed as a board-tracker and would make its debut at the motordrome; its name certainly awakened images of a new wind on the saucer tracks. In addition, newspaper reports of road and dirt-track races around the same time do not mention the machine. Joerns itself did not mention the Cyclone in its ads or in the St. Paul city directory until 1915.

No matter the exact date of introduction, the Cyclone was the most technically advanced motorcycle of its era in the United States—and probably the world.

1989 SUZUKI GSX-R750RR
Suzuki was a builder of weaving machinery before it branched out following World War II to offer a bicycle fitted with a 36-cc two-stroke auxiliary engine. In 1985, the firm established itself at the top rung of race-replica superbike builders with its GSX-R750, featuring oil cooling and an aluminum-alloy frame. This was the production racer "RR" version. Owner: Bill Peters.

"Riding His Cyclone Like a Madman"

On Saturday, June 21, 1914, McNeil won the first race he entered with the Cyclone, breaking the track 3-mile (4.8-km) record en route. The St. Paul Pioneer Press's headline was to be echoed many times over the summer: "Riding a Cyclone for First Time, Salt Lake Man is Easy Winner."

On Wednesday, June 24, McNeil and the Cyclone shattered the 2-mile (3.2-km) record and won one heat of a three-heat race over pro rider Larry Fleckenstein aboard his factory Indian. Again, on Sunday, June 29, McNeil and the Cyclone broke the motordrome's 1-mile (1.6-km) record with a speed 97.29 mph (156.9 km) on his way to winning five heats and races. On Wednesday, July 1, McNeil and the Cyclone broke the 2-mile (3.2-km) record and won five more heats and races.

On Saturday night, July 4, McNeil and the Cyclone broke the world's 4-mile (6.5-km) record for quarter-mile (400-m) motordromes and was within one and a half seconds of the world's record for a 1-mile (1.6-km) straightaway. Along the way that evening, he won six heats and races.

On Wednesday, July 8, McNeil broke the 2-mile (3.2-km) record "riding his Cyclone racing machine like a madman," reported the St. Paul Pioneer Press. Throughout the summer, the duo continued to win heats and races at the Twin City Motordrome against tough competition, including Fleckenstein and Curly Fredricks.

McNeil took the Cyclone to the St. Louis (Missouri) Motordrome in the first part of July but was barred from racing there. For the remainder of the summer, he almost owned the Twin City Motordrome, winning many of the heats he entered and besting his own speed records.

Later in 1914, Fleckenstein parked his Indian and joined longtime rival McNeil on a Cyclone at the new Omaha, Nebraska, motordrome. McNeil ran a mile (1.6-km) dash in 32.4 seconds for a record speed of an astonishing 111.1 mph (179.2-kph), far beyond the recognized world record of 93.48 mph (150.8 kph) set by Englishman S. George on an Indian and Excelsior's Lee Humiston's 100-mph (161.3-kph) mark. But the Federation of American Motorcyclists (FAM) refused to recognize the Cyclone's achievement; as Jerry Hatfield noted in his landmark book American Racing Motorcycles: The FAM was "doubtless being suspicious of such a high speed margin over other motorcycles of the time."

In 1915, McNeil was hired away from Joerns to serve as development engineer at Excelsior, and his place was eagerly taken by veteran board-tracker Don Johns. On January 31, 1915, Johns appeared with his new Cyclone at the 1-mile dirt track in Ascot, California, for a 100-mile (161.2-km) race. During the day's prelude race, Johns chalked up a new 10-mile (16.1-km) record at 8:14. But it was in the 100-miler that Johns established the Cyclone indelibly in the minds of the established rivals from Indian, Excelsior, and Harley-Davidson. Johns blazed away from the field, lapping every other rider before dirt

1996 APRILIA RS250

A former bicycle maker, Aprilia of Noale, Italy, did not begin to build motorized two-wheelers until 1960. By 1982, the firm committed itself to challenging the might of the Japanese makers in Grand Prix racing, eventually winning its first 125-cc season in 1992. Aprilia's premier racers were powered by Austrian Rotax engines before in-house development created the current breed of two-strokes. By 1994, Aprilia finally wore the 250-cc World Championship crown due to the heroic antics of rider Max Biaggi. Owner: Jimmy Lin.

clogged his carburetor at the 50-mile (80.7-km) mark and forced him out.

Other riders sought glory aboard the Cyclone in 1915 as well, including D. O. "Dave" Kinnie, Bill Goudy, Carl Eschereich, and a rider known simply as "Fabian." At the July 4 300-mile (483.9-km) National Championship in Dodge City, Kansas, Kinnie set the fastest lap in qualifying at 88.5 mph (142.7-kph), although Johns and his Cyclone retaliated with a 90-mph (145.2-kph) lap during the race. As *Motorcycle Illustrated* enthused: "Johns' work was nothing short of spectacular and it was generally understood that he was gaiting himself for a new 100-mile record." Unfortunately, about three-quarters of the way through the race, Johns's Cyclone faltered, and he lost the lead, eventually retiring along with Kinnie.

In 1916, Johns returned to Indian, but Kinnie and other privateers continued to wave the Cyclone flag. Kinnie won a 10-mile (16.1-km) pro race at Stockton, California, on June 20 before following Johns's lead in joining Indian.

MAKING HISTORY

Engineering the development, production, sales, and support of a new motorcycle marque—as well as operating a national racing team—was a Herculean effort at the best of times. The challenge was too much, and on October 19, 1915, Joerns announced that it was ceasing motorcycle production. The Cyclone was no more.

Joerns had done battle as David against the Goliath of the established Indian, Excelsior, and Harley-Davidson factories for two years. Earlier in 1915, it had debuted two production models alongside its factory racers: the roadgoing "Model 7, C-15" and the privateer racer's "Model 7, R-15 Stripped Stock Model." The number of Cyclones built and sold during the one to two years of production has never been established; only a handful exist today.

Motorcycle historian Hatfield traces the Cyclone's history following Joerns's closure: In 1916, a group of Chicago investors bought Joerns's assets with grand plans to revive the Cyclone. The plans never materialized, and the group sold out to two partners, who moved the operation to Cheboygan, Michigan, in 1920. In 1920–1921, another group rumored to be associated with General Motors bought the assets and built a factory in Benton Harbor, Michigan, but again production plans faltered. In 1923, the Reading-Standard Company raced a Cyclone copy based on engine castings purchased from Joerns. And with that, the Cyclone name was finally laid to rest.

The Twin City Motordrome was also razed after the decline of board-track racing in 1916 following a series of horrific accidents and deaths at saucer tracks around the United States. Preachers and journalists and concerned do-gooders joined voices in shouting down the brief spectacle that was motordrome racing. By the dawn of World War I, it was all history.

The sport of racing merits special consideration whether in and of itself or whether for its singular values. This sport that you cultivate requires a certain force of character, a harmonious force of the whole body whose energy manifests itself above all in the loyalty and in the disciplines of life. But more efficacious and more exalted is the reality of your symbolic race toward the glory of eternal life. Since you are loyal to the Christian life and you want to conquer not just a trophy that can be passed on to other hands, but a holy, indestructible crown.
—Pope Pius XII speaking to motorcycle racers, 1950s

Chapter 4

DAREDEVILS

FROM LUCKY LEE LOTT TO EVEL KNIEVEL

HAPPY DAREDEVILS, 1941
ABOVE: *Lucky Lee Lott, left, and fellow Hell Driver Rocky Decker looked slightly dazed but happy as they stood in front of yet another burning wreck in Stratford, Ontario. Football helmets were de rigueur safety protection; ropes or chains padded by pillows served as seatbelts. (Photograph from Lucky Lee Lott Archives)*

"HELL ON WHEELS"
LEFT: *Garish and gaudy were the keys to luring folks in to see the marvels of a Wall of Death. This poster promised chills and spills—as the Angel of Death watched from the front row.*

It was 1935, and twenty-year-old Lee Lott of Pekin, Illinois, wanted to spread his wings. He was ready to gamble his savings from selling vacuum cleaners door to door. Lee was getting into the daredevil business.

Lee had grand dreams of crashing cycles and cars in front of adoring crowds, so he gathered several of his buddies around the kitchen table—including his fourteen-year-old brother and his life-long friend Lou "Batter" Crooks—and began making plans. The first thing they needed was a name. "Satan's Pals" had a ring to it, even if it was slightly incongruous. They plotted to paint their cars and motor-cycles pale white as though they were cemetery ghosts; their new moniker would be written in garish red, dripping down like fresh blood.

Now they needed some cars to wreck. They bought two crashed Fords from a junkyard—a Tudor that was half burnt out but still ran, and a Fordor that had been rolled. Batter was handy with a sledge-hammer, so he got to work and punched the roof back out on the four-door. Then he lit up his welding torch and added some reinforc-ing pipes and welded all of the doors shut. This was going to be the fledgling outfit's "roll car." Batter had his Harley-Davidson that would come in handy for jumps, and Lee had a DeSoto Airflow that could also be put to use.

Lee got permission from a local farmer to use his pasture for practice, and Satan's Pals started learning how to be daredevils the hard way. Using a 6-foot (1.8-m) length of baling wire wrapped in a leather jacket as a safety belt, they practiced rolling their roll car. On his first attempt, Batter actually got it to roll twice—although the second roll was accidental, and he wound up face down in the dirt. His carefully considered comment afterward was, "That's like doing a high dive without any water in the pool."

At night, Lee put the kitchen table back to work as a drafting board and designed ramps and blocks for jumping their cycles and cars. During the days, Lee drove around town with a speaker mounted to the roof of his newly painted DeSoto announcing the debut show on the Fourth of July, promising "Thrills, spills, and free parking." The crew kept on practicing, earning their degree in daredev-ilry from the school of hard knocks.

A SHOW IS BORN

The day of the big show finally arrived. With their rented

FLYING HARLEY, 1950S
Practice session for Lucky Lee Lott's Hell Drivers. (Photograph from Lucky Lee Lott Archives)

pasture tarted up with banners and binder twine strung from fence posts to hold back the expected crowd, Satan's Pals stood around their Harley waiting for an audience. The show was set for 2:00 P.M., but 1:00 P.M. came and went with the pasture still empty. At 1:30, Satan's Pals were still watching the alfalfa grow. Then, just before Lee's watch struck 2:00, an Illinois Highway State Trooper pulled up.

"Who runs this outfit," the trooper demanded.

Lee's voice cracked, "I'll have to take the blame, but we're waiting for customers."

The officer responded, "If you'd open that gate, I'll help you get them in."

Satan's Pals had forgotten to open the field's gate, which was out of sight and out of mind over the hill from the pasture.

The trooper continued, "You've got a backup of traffic 4 miles [6.5 km] to the light in Kewanee and 5 miles [8.1 km] down to Route 91. Let's get with it."

Lee hightailed it over to the gate, feverishly opening it as he looked over his shoulder to a line of cars stretching away as far as his eyes could see. Within minutes, their 500 tickets were gone, and the cars kept rolling in, leaving the gatekeepers with nothing to do but stuff dollar bills into their pockets. Soon the parking lot was full, so Lee leased the next field over from the farmer for the price of the soybean crop, and the crowd continued to roll in.

At 3:00 P.M., Lee put the "Comedian's Gallop" on the turntable, and with apologies to all, the show swung into action. Lee kicked it off with the Two-Wheel Drive, revving his DeSoto onto a ramp, lifting two wheels off the ground, and piloting it the length of the pasture. Then came the Slide for Life with one of the Pals hanging onto the rear bumper, sliding along behind the car through a patch of burning gas. Next was the Human Battering Ram, with another one of the

HEADSTAND, 1920S

A pioneer daredevil stands on his head on an Indian single. Riding while doing a headstand might not be too tough: The question was how to get into that riding position.

1928 Harley-Davidson JDH Two Cam

For a brief spell in 1928 and 1929, Harley-Davidson released a hot-rod version of the JD with two cams in place of the standard solo camshaft. The 74-ci (1,212-cc) JDH was a true sleeper: Only a revised camshaft cover hinted at the extra power, and many unwary Indian riders found themselves eating the dust of what looked like another ordinary streetbike. Owner: Eldon Brown.

devil's finest tied head-first on the hood of the Ford and driven through a board wall set aflame. Then came the Blindfold Jump.

The crowd waited in silent anticipation as Batter sat astride his Harley while Lee tied a blindfold around his helmetless head. He kicked the V-twin to life, gassed it a couple times, and then rooster-tailed down the pasture. He took one quick peak from under the blindfold to make certain he had the Milwaukee Marvel lined up right, and then gunned the engine. He came roaring past the crowd and onto the 7.5-foot-high (2.3-m) wooden ramp that sent him soaring through the air to crash into a burning wall of wood and excelsior. The flames engulfed him as he split through the wall with his head tucked down like a battering ram. Batter and his Harley landed and bounced a couple times. But something felt wrong; the cycle was on fire. Feeling a bit warm, Batter abandoned the flaming Harley at full throttle and dove—still blindfolded—for the safety of the alfalfa. The riderless cycle careened down the field afire until it tipped over and flipped. Another Pal rushed to the scene with a bucket of water.

When a bent and charred Batter struggled to his feet and threw off his blindfold, the crowd went crazy.

A show was born.

Daredevil Iron

From that day forward, Lee gained the nickname "Lucky" Lee Lott, and the show soon changed its moniker to the Hell Drivers. He used his share from that first show to buy gas and bologna sandwiches, and they started touring the United States and Canada. By the late 1940s,

PAULINE'S PERILS, 1940S

RIGHT: *Actress Betty Hutton risked life and limb in a Hollywood studio to climb from her faithful Indian into an airplane. It was all in a day's work while filming the long-running movie serial,* The Perils of Pauline.

LOW-RENT DAREDEVIL, 1938

BELOW: *Before setting up this daring jump in Edmonton, Alberta, the prone accomplices must have drawn straws to see who laid down where. The long-straw holder was most likely the one nearest the landing pad. (Photograph from City of Edmonton Archives)*

71

the Lucky Lee Lott Hell Drivers was the largest daredevil show in the world.

Lee signed a deal with the then-big-deal Nash car company to use and abuse its products before crowds everywhere. Lee jumped cars into lakes, drove Ford Tri-Motor airplanes into houses, and set a world record in 1942 by jumping a car 169 feet (51.5 m). By the time Lucky Lee Lott retired from putting on his Gasoline Opera, he had laid 17,981 cars to eternal rest.

Retired in Florida these days, Lee is still tallying how many motorcycles he and his pals destroyed. From the 1930s through the 1950s, the Hell Drivers were leaping cycles over one to a dozen cars, battering motorcycles through flaming board walls—blindfolded or not—crashing through walls of 28-gauge furnace steel, riding through 30-foot-long (9.2-m) burning tunnels, jumping over fellow Hell Drivers laid side by side, and crashing cycles head-on into cars. They were tricks that needed more than just bottled courage. As Lee put it, the top-notch motorcycle daredevil required three essential components: balance, bravery, and continence.

In his three decades of daredevilry, Lucky Lee Lott went through a lot of front forks and other front-end components. He also went through a lot of motorcycles, period. The Hell Drivers typically bought their cycles from finance companies that had repossessed the bikes from their "owners." They also picked up crashed cycles on the cheap from insurance companies, sorted out the good parts, and made one cycle out of two, or three, or four.

"I always kept my eye out for a Harley-Davidson, Milwaukee's finest," Lee recollected, "and performed many a stunt on that good Wisconsin Iron.

"The best motorcycle for the Head-On Crash was a Henderson Four, which we tracked down once upon a time. The Henderson was just built well. It was something solid and dependable beneath you when you lined up against a speeding car for the Head-On.

"One of my motorcycle stuntmen, Joe Langford, had an English-built Ariel Red Hunter for a time, and that was a good cycle for balance acts. We also once found a 1947 Ariel Square Four up in Canada, and my riders Steve Stiles and Ron Childers used it for their acts for several years. That Ariel was a delightful machine."

But just as Lee swore by Nash cars, there was one motorcycle that stood head and shoulders above all others for daredevilry: the Indian Scout.

"Wall of Death riders loved it for their circus and fair sideshows

"DARE DEVIL GIRLS," 1952
A dynamic daredevil duo at the Edmonton Exhibition drew in the crowd with their fearless feline. The thrills were performed on every daredevil's favorite mount, the tried and true Indian Scout. (Photograph from Provincial Archives of Alberta)

for the same reasons we did: The Scout was lightweight yet perfectly balanced," recounted Lee. The chassis was setup just right, but above all, the Indian's V-twin engine was balanced, nearly vibrationless, and simply kept on ticking despite all of the Human Battering Rams, Flaming Wall Crashes, and Ten-Car jumps.

Lucky Lee Lott lauds the V-twin Indian Scout with his highest praise: "It was the ideal machine for a head stand."

JUMPING BOXES OF RATTLESNAKES

While Lucky Lee Lott and crew were on top of the daredevil world doing headstands on their Indians and crashing Nashes in more ways than dreamed possible, a young punk named Robert Craig Knievel was stealing hubcaps in Butte, Montana. A copper-mining boomtown, Butte was notorious as one of the roughest, toughest cities on earth. This was the wild, wild West, circa the 1940s. From around the world, the mines lured immigrants with an eye on the American Dream, and Bob's family was one of many who came West with dollar signs in their eyes. In the 1940s, pilfering hubcaps was a typical endeavor for young Bob to keep himself in cigarettes, beer, and pocket change. As one victim swore at him, "You're a little evil, Knievel." Bob liked the way that rang and kept it filed in the back of his mind for a later date.

Growing up in Butte, Bob had only one legitimate choice for his future: work the mines. To let off steam after five days of working for The Man, Bob kickstarted his Triumph motorcycle and raced dirt tracks and motocross. Now and then, he rode broncos in the rodeo, played ice hockey, sold insurance, robbed banks and drug stores—anything to make a buck. It was a good way to relax on a weekend—washed down on a Saturday night with a cold beer and Rocky Mountain oysters.

In the early 1960s, Bob broke away from Butte and moved on to greener pastures. He ran a string of motorcycle shops first in Butte, then in Spokane and Moses Lake, Washington, where he plowed out a dirt-track raceway. He needed a gimmick to sell all those shiny new bikes gathering dust in the shop front, so Bob figured he would put on a special attraction of his own at the weekend races.

The grandstands were packed to bursting that weekend with 1,000 or so hard-core spectators happy to watch anyone do just about anything with a motorcycle. Bob aimed to please. He revved his Norton, rooster-tailed down the dirt track, up onto a homebuilt wooden ramp, and set sail on his first jump. He only flew about 40 feet (12 m) on that first leap, but distance wasn't everything. Bob was jumping his motorcycle over a big box filled with rattlesnakes—with a mountain lion staked at each end for good measure. Even with his first stunt, he knew how to capture the public's attention.

Unfortunately, being his first airborne performance and all, things didn't go quite as planned. Forty feet wasn't enough to clear the rattler box, and his Norton crashed through the far end. Bob was OK; it was the crowd that got worked up. As the rattlesnakes escaped, Bob's first fans took to their heels and ran for the hills.

Bob, meanwhile, was laughing all the way to the bank—although it's not clear how many motorcycles the stunt sold.

EVEL KNIEVEL, 1970S
From a volatile boyhood to ice hockey star, insurance salesman to motorcycle daredevil, Evel Knievel embodied the American Dream. He was unique among heroes: He was a living, breathing Superman, able to leap a lineup of Mack trucks in a single bound. These days, the Evel legend still looms, kept alive by his own website, www.evel.com. (Photograph from Evel and Kelly Knievel)

THE BIRTH OF EVEL KNIEVEL

From that day forward, things only got better. At a fairgrounds in Palm Springs, California, Bob jumped a couple trucks. Soon, he and his flying Norton became a standard feature at county fairs and motorcycle races up and down the coast.

Then in Barstow, he hit the big time—and hit it the hard way. He was debuting a new act, wherein a buddy drove a motorcycle straight at him at full bore only to have Bob leap straight up in the air and just clear the bike at the last possible moment. The act worked well in practice, but in front of the crowd in Barstow his timing was off. The speeding cycle hit him just where it hurt the most, and Bob flipped to the ground like a discarded rag doll. But it was getting hurt in a crazy, senseless, brutal way that won attention: All the newspapers carried a photo of Bob Knievel unconscious and broken on the Barstow pavement. Suddenly, his name was big and everyone wanted to book his show.

When he was back on his feet, Bob set up shop in Hollywood for "Bob Knievel and his Motorcycle Daredevils," offering a two-and-a-half-hour show of thrills and spills. Bob had all the requisites for a great show in the grand old barnstorming circus tradition: He had a hired midget, he popped wheelies, and he jumped his cycle as the grand finale.

The problem was he was learning as he jumped, meaning he frequently crashed. When he was laid up in the hospital, he still had to write checks to his midget and the rest of the crew even though he was the main draw and the one who took all the knocks. Bob soon realized that no one was coming to see the midget; they were coming to see Bob Knievel, and the more death-defying, the more dangerous the stunt, the better. Bloodthirstiness never seems to go out of fashion.

The next time he jumped his cycle, he was no longer Bob Knievel. He harkened back to his good old hubcap-stealing days and took on that crime victim's curse as a full-time moniker. From then on, he would be Evel Knievel.

THE DAREDEVIL ELVIS

Evel Knievel could jump just about anything on his cycle. He lept over rows of cars, a tank full of sharks, and once, over thirteen Mack trucks in Toronto.

He had traded in his Norton and gotten sponsorship from a fledging importer called American Eagle, which brought in shiploads of Laverda 750 cycles from Italy, slapped its own decal on the tank, and sold the Italian cycle under the patriotic banner. For a couple years, these American Eagle–badged Laverdas were his jump of choice. Then, he was handed a thoroughbred American jumping machine, the cycle he became known by, a full-bore Harley-Davidson XR-750. The cycle was given to him by Harley-Davidson, which certainly knew the benefit of publicity.

Evel had style. Decked out in a red, white, and blue Elvis Presley–

Color me lucky.
—Evel Knievel

style jumpsuit with a Superman cape and a king's gold-headed scepter, Evel lined up his motorcycle straight and true, and made the big jump with no gimmicks, no smoke, no mirrors. He was the real thing. The superlative had not been invented that could truly describe him. At a time when the country was splitting apart in a million directions, Evel Knievel was doing what made America great: living dangerously by his wits, challenging the authority of gravity, crafting P. T. Barnum–style spectacle. He was a self-made man earning the American Dream in the most outrageous manner ever dreamed possible. He was John Wayne on wheels, a daredevil Elvis, Bogart with a helmet, JFK with pointy sideburns, a household hero, an original, all-American 1960s cool.

Evel had his own Learjets, Ferraris, yachts, thoroughbred horses, houses, and women galore. There were Evel Knievel toys, cologne, and several movies made of his life.

Evel could jump just about anything. Problem was, the landings often hurt. He could always buy another motorcycle to jump, but he was stuck with his own body. During his career, he broke thirty-five bones and suffered through fifteen major operations to rebuild "components" such as a shattered hip and pelvis, insert aluminum plates to hold his arms together, and simply stitch him back together.

On New Year's Eve 1967, he jumped the fountain at Caesar's Palace casino in Las Vegas only to crash and bounce across the pavement like a rag doll. The crash crushed his pelvis, broke his femurs, and left him in a coma for twenty-nine days. But he bounced back.

On September 8, 1974, he tried to jump the Snake River Canyon in Idaho in front of millions of TV viewers. His 13-foot-long (4-meter), rocket-powered Skyrocket X-2 shot off with Evel riding it like an astronaut. He flew 1,000 feet (300 meters) into the air before an auxiliary parachute accidentally blew open, halting his forward progress, and the wind carried him ignominiously back toward his launching pad. He crashed 600 feet (180 meters) below the canyon rim and bounced to a rest at the edge of the river. A paramedic team airlifted him by helicopter to a hospital. The jump was a bust, but Evel still pocketed $6 million from the failure.

This time he didn't bounce back, however. After the failed Snake River jump and all the hoopla surrounding it, his name became tarnished. To all those TV viewers, that jump was a huge disappointment. What goes up, must come down, and Evel Knievel was on his downward trajectory.

One day, en route to a show in Texas, Evel and his crew were grabbing lunch at a cafe in Deming, New Mexico, when he overhead two locals swapping tall tales of his own exploits. "He's jumped 152 cars," one said, stretching the truth out to the horizon. "The Grand Canyon, too," the other countered, not to be outdone.

As Evel Knievel himself later told it, he realized then and there that he was going to kill himself trying to live up to his own legend.

THE LEGENDS LIVE ON

Daredevilry is not a job from which it is easy to retire with grace. Evel Knievel was famous when he was in midair, but Bob Knievel had to deal with the landing. "I came to a point in my life where I just couldn't pull the gun out of my holster anymore," Evel said. "I just couldn't do it. I couldn't pull the trigger. I'd been hurt some thirty times, and every time I was driving my car and saw a bus or a truck coming down the road I used to wince. It's something you can't explain, but believe me, it gets to you."

Evel still has his bent and broken body to contend with, as well as life-threatening hepatitis C from one too many blood transfusions. And then, despite a lifetime's worth of warnings not to follow in the old man's footsteps, Evel Knievel's own son, Robbie, became a daredevil and began breaking his father's records. In April 1989, Robbie successfully leaped the Caesar's Palace fountains, which added insult to an old, slow-healing injury. In February 1998, he outdid his dad's distance record, jumping over thirty Tropicana Hotel limousines with a 230-foot (70-meter) leap. He broke Evel's record by one measly foot (30 cm).

What does a motorcycle daredevil have to hold onto once all the exhaust fumes have wafted away and the cheers of many crowds have echoed into silence? As Lucky Lee Lott wrote in his autobiography, "If he's alive, that's a lot to be thankful for. Of course I have a crooked back from one too many jumps and ears that still ring from a dynamite stunt once upon a time ago.

"And then there are the memories: 17,981 cars crashed, smashed, and destroyed in various others means as well as hundreds of motorcycles, fourteen airplanes, and a few dozen speedboats—all of which provide many tales for the telling."

The only thing that lasts is the legend.

YET ANOTHER BROKEN RECORD . . .
This poster from the Ontario Motor Speedway in California bid all motorcycle fans to watch their hero break yet another record, this time jumping no less than nineteen Dodges. Over the years, the daredevil records fell like bowling pins beneath Evel Knievel's cycle.

Chapter 5

THE
HARLEY-DAVIDSON–
INDIAN WARS

THE BATTLE FOR THE HEART OF AMERICAN MOTORCYCLISTS

TRYING AN INDIAN ON FOR SIZE, 1917

ABOVE: *Junior tests the comfort of the pillion behind Pa on the family's Indian V-twin in Bremner, Alberta. (Photograph from Provincial Archives of Alberta)*

1936 HARLEY-DAVIDSON 61 OHV MODEL EL

LEFT: *The arrival of Harley-Davidson's overhead-valve Big Twin inspired ecstasy among dealers—one of whom saw fit to unleash a fusillade of bullets from his six-gun into the air at the unveiling in pure, unadulterated glee. Such contagious celebration seems fitting today in hindsight as the Knucklehead became the secret weapon that won the war with Indian—and evolved into the engine that powers Harleys to this day. Owner: Carman Brown.*

The day the tide turned in the three-decades-long war between Harley-Davidson and Indian was a time for celebration. The battle between the two dominant motorcycle makers had been the central theme of American motorcycling. Now, with the debut of Harley's forthcoming Model 61 OHV, the Milwaukee faithful had a new secret weapon.

The Harley dealers were enraptured. At the dealers' banquet after the first unveiling of the new machine at Milwaukee's Schroeder Hotel on November 25, 1935, the celebration quickly went over the top. "Cactus" Bill Kennedy, a cowboy Harley dealer from Phoenix, Arizona, was so elated that he pulled his revolver in the middle of the dining hall and "he [drew] a bead on the crystal chandelier, let out a blood-curdling yip-eee . . . and emptie[d] his six-gun," enthused *The Enthusiast*, Harley's house magazine. The more sedate dealers merely passed out after imbibing one toast too many of Milwaukee's finest brews. It was a day that went down in Harley history.

At the time, the long-awaited overhead-valve motorcycle seemed like a fine tool to win back flagging sales from Harley's archrival amidst the Great Depression. To the men in orange and black, that was reason enough to drink Milwaukee dry and gun down an innocent chandelier.

In hindsight, however, the event marked the turning point that would make the Milwaukee company the victor after battling for years on the racetracks, sales floors, and drawing boards.

A CONTRACT ON AN OLD ENVELOPE

In January 1901, George M. Hendee of Springfield, Massachusetts, scrawled out a contract on the back of an old envelope putting his faith in his new-found acquaintance, Oscar Hedstrom, to build the future in the form of a motorized bicycle. Hendee and Hedstrom had one thing in common: They were both former bicycle racers who saw the future not in pedal power but in mechanical power.

From there, they were very different men. In the late 1880s, Hendee had retired from racing and established the Hendee Manufacturing Company in Springfield to build his Silver King bicycles during the booming years of the bicycle craze. Hendee was the money man; he had deep pockets that could make things happen.

Hedstrom was the idea man. In 1899, he was at New York City's Madison Square Garden when Frenchman Henri Fournier's motorized tandem bicycle paced a bicycle race. By the end of the year, Hedstrom had schooled himself in the

PROUD INDIAN RIDERS, 1905
Motorcycle gangs seemed to form as soon as two riders met up, as evidenced by this group with their early Indian singles standing in front of a Minneapolis, Minnesota, Indian dealership.

newfangled gas-powered internal-combustion engine and crafted his own motorized pacer. In 1900, Hendee witnessed Hedstrom and his pacer at work, and an idea was born.

With the ink still drying on their contract written on the old envelope, Hedstrom rented space at the Worcester Bicycle Manufacturing Company in Middletown, Connecticut, and got down to work. Armed with a full machine shop, bicycles and bicycle components, and photographs and drawings of original ideas and other machines he had seen, Hedstrom crafted a motorized bicycle that could be sold to the public. Fifteen months later, in May 1901, Hedstrom wired Hendee that the prototype for what would become the Indian "motocycle" was ready.

The first Indians of 1901 and 1902 were for all practical purposes motorized bicycles. They were built on a modified bicycle chassis of a diamond-shaped frame with the motor bolted onto the seat tube. Chain drive ran from the engine's output shaft to the bicycle's front chain ring, which retained crank arms and pedals for starting.

The engine was a solid and reliable 15.85-ci (264.2-cc) F-head single that dutifully pumped out 1.75 hp. A gas tank was added atop

1906 INDIAN SINGLE

George Hendee and Oscar Hedstrom's premier Indian of 1901 was a landmark machine of its day. It bore such an influential design that copies of the Indian were available from motorcycle makers everywhere. The Indian was powered by a 15.85-ci (260-cc) F-head single-cylinder engine that dutifully pumped out 2¼ hp. It was fitted into a bicycle chassis, which was handy as the Hendee Manufacturing Company of Springfield, Massachusetts, also built Silver King bicycles. This Indian model remained in production until 1908, but its influences were felt for decades after. Owner: Reynolds-Alberta Museum.

1914 INDIAN HENDEE SPECIAL

The Hendee Special was regarded with awe when it was unveiled in 1914. Here was a vision of the motorcycle of tomorrow, complete with electric starter and lights as well as Indian's tried and true 61-ci (1,000-cc) V-twin engine creating 7 hp. Sadly, electrical batteries of the day were notoriously unreliable, tarnishing the image of the Hendee Special and spelling its doom after only one year of production. Owner: Peter Gagan.

the rear fender, and lubricating oil arrived via a drip feed. The machine weighed in at 75 pounds (34.1 kg). The engine could be throttled back to a walking speed of 3 mph (4.8 kph) or up to a startling full-out speed of more than 30 mph (48 kph)—a heady speed in those days.

It was a simple yet solid machine, and the Indian soon became one of the best known, most prolific, and most influential motorcycles anywhere.

BORN IN A SHED

The story of the creation of the Harley-Davidson in a shed behind the Davidson family's Milwaukee home has become legend, akin to that of the birth of a certain baby in a manger some 2,000 years ago. Twenty-one-year-old William S. Harley and his childhood pal, twenty-

year-old Arthur Davidson, were enamored by the newfangled motorcycles being built by others, but they thought they could do better. They worked at a Milwaukee manufacturing firm, where Harley was an apprentice draftsman and Davidson a pattern maker. The duo met a German draftsman at work who regaled them with tales of the pioneering European motor bicycles. With his help, Harley and Davidson drafted plans for a single-cylinder gas-fueled engine that followed the style set by Count de Dion and Georges Bouton. In the evenings starting in 1901, they worked in their home basement, building a scaled-down prototype motor-cycle.

But the duo was struggling with their creation. They had pooled their less-than-ideal engineering knowledge to build the machine: Harley had previously crafted his own bicycle in his spare time, and Davidson's pattern-making skills came in handy. What they needed was a mechanic.

So, Arthur wrote to his brother Walter, who was a top-notch machinist and worked in the tool room for a Kansas railroad. Arthur painted a glowing picture of their motorcycle and offered Walter a ride on the new machine when he was home in Milwaukee for the wedding of a third Davidson brother, William. As Walter later remembered, "Imagine my chagrin to find that the moto bicycle in question had reached the stage of blueprints, and before I could have the promised ride, I had to help finish the machine." Still, he was intrigued and saw promise in the duo's design. He quit his railroad job, rolled up his shirtsleeves, and got down to work. After his wedding, William, a toolmaker, also joined in.

The first engine measured 2.125x2.875 inches (54.5x73.7 mm), displacing 25 ci (417 cc). It was fed by a carburetor reportedly fashioned from a recycled tomato can. Unfortunately, the engine did not produce enough power, so a second was built in 1902, increased to

Potato–potato–potato. —The sound of an idling Harley-Davidson V-twin, according to Harley's trademark attorney Joseph Bonk, who was involved in filing the sound with the U.S. Patent and Trademark Office in 1994

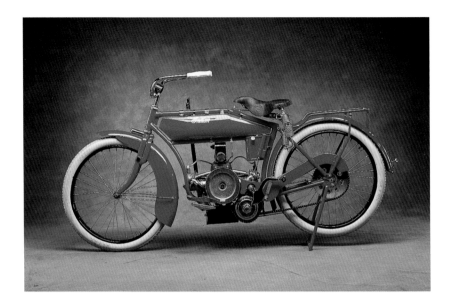

1917 Indian Light Twin Model O

A road not traveled: Indian experimented with a small-bore, horizontally opposed twin from 1917 to 1919, but the market proved minuscule. The 15.7-ci (257-cc) side-valve engine created 4 hp. Owner: Clifford Zimmerman.

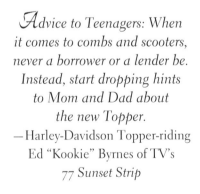

Advice to Teenagers: When it comes to combs and scooters, never a borrower or a lender be. Instead, start dropping hints to Mom and Dad about the new Topper.
—Harley-Davidson Topper-riding Ed "Kookie" Byrnes of TV's *77 Sunset Strip*

3.00x3.50 inches (76.2x88.9 mm) and producing a muscular 3 hp. The tomato-can carburetor was set aside after friend Ole Evinrude, who would later find fame building outboard motors, helped design and build a "real" carb.

For a frame, they tried first a typical bicycle diamond frame like the one Oscar Hedstrom was using. But this frame could not hold the engine's power, so they crafted a loop frame, a design that would be a Harley-Davidson staple for decades.

With their prototype now running, Walter finally took his long-promised ride. He pronounced it a sound machine.

Now that they had a running prototype, the friends decided to enter production. The Davidsons' father, William C., was a cabinet-maker by trade. Inspired by his sons' machine, he constructed a 10x15-foot (3.1x4.6-m) shed in the family's backyard that would become their first "factory." The friends painted their new company's name on the door: "Harley-Davidson Motor Co." Bill Harley received top billing because he had engineered the first prototype.

In 1903, two or three motor bicycles were built, followed by two or three more in 1904. By 1905, production had more than doubled to seven. The first Harley was sold before it was finished to a local man named Meyer, who put 6,000 miles (9,655 km) on the machine before selling it to a George Lyon, who added 15,000 miles (24,140 km). It then went through three more owners and traveled 62,000 additional miles (100,000 km). Harley-Davidson proudly advertised in 1913 that that first machine had more than 100,000 miles (161,000 km) under its belt.

THE BATTLE FOR SURVIVAL

The battle in the early years was simply for survival, and at first, Indian and Harley-Davidson did not view themselves as true competitors. The "motocycle" was a newfangled invention and not everyone cottoned to it. The two firms focused on establishing themselves.

Harley-Davidson was quietly building a reputation for stoic

reliability. The fledgling company did not support racing throughout its first decade, choosing instead to prove its machine on the road. The only notable exceptions to this policy were a pair of prestigious victories won by company president Walter Davidson in 1908. First, he won the two-day endurance run through New York State sanctioned by the Federation of American Motorcyclists (FAM), scoring a perfect 1,000 points. A week later, he won the FAM-sanctioned economy run on Long Island, New York, with a fuel-consumption average of 188 mpg (78.8 kpl). These victories gave Harley-Davidson national stature.

Harley-Davidson also was a staunch defender of quiet motorcycles. It campaigned to muffle the roar of motorcycle exhaust, pointing out in its ads that it fixed large mufflers to its machines so they would not scare horses or the unsuspecting pedestrian. From this "quiet pipes save lives" campaign, the early Harleys won the name Silent Gray Fellow, as they were quiet and usually painted in gray. The "Fellow" part of the nickname originated from Harley-Davidson's promoting its motorcycle as reliable companion on the lonesome road. Then as now, Harley-Davidson was concerned about its image.

Indian, meanwhile, was attacking all markets, perhaps because it didn't have a clear idea in those days of where a motorcycle fit in, so the firm saw it fitting everywhere in the brave new world. At country-

1912 HARLEY-DAVIDSON "SILENT GRAY FELLOW"

The "Silent Gray Fellow" moniker was baptized on Harley-Davidson's early singles by the Milwaukee company as a kind of advertising slogan. "Silent" promoted the quiet-running, 30-ci (492-cc) engine that pumped out 6.5 hp. "Gray" was Harley's signature paint scheme. "Fellow" denoted the reliability of the machine, which would faithfully serve its owner as a good friend and fellow should. Owner: Reynolds-Alberta Museum.

fair horseracing tracks and on the board-track motordromes, Indians were duking it out with Excelsiors, Flying Merkels, and Reading Standards in bloody battles for race trophies.

On the salesroom floors of the nation, however, Indian's main competition was itself—or at least a shadow of itself. As the Indian was the most influential motorcycle in North America, it naturally inspired copies.

From 1902 to 1907, Indian contracted the Aurora Manufacturing Company of Aurora, Illinois, to build its engines because Indian did not have the manufacturing capacity needed. As part of the deal, Aurora could use or sell any excess engines Indian did not require, so it launched its own motorcycle, the Thor, using not only the same engine as the Indian but an exact duplicate design in all other respects as well.

Other firms also bought the Aurora-built engine and soon launched their own Indian clones, including the Light, Light Thor-Bred, and Thor-Bred motorcycles from the Light Manufacturing & Foundry Company of Pottstown, Pennsylvania, forerunner of the Merkel firm; the DeLong from the Industrial Machine Company of Phoenix, New York; the America from the Great Western Manufacturing Company of LaPorte, Indiana; the Warwick Motor Cycle; the Apache from Brown & Beck of Denver, Colorado; and the Manson from the Fowler-Sherman-Manson Cycle Company of Chicago. There were undoubtedly more.

Copying was rampant in the pioneering days of motorcycles. Some machines were blatant duplicates of original machines made without the approval of the maker. Sometimes this copying was in the form of "inspiration": An original engine design provided the concept, and perhaps the measurements, for another engineer. Some makers applied for patents on their creations, but the granting of a patent often took years. And even if the design was patented, actual patent protection was another matter altogether.

News traveled slowly in the 1900s, and product distribution was often even slower. This created an environment where inventors such as Harley and the Davidsons could release its copy of an engine originally built by Count de Dion and Georges Bouton in France, and the original makers might never even hear of the copycat machine and attempt to put on the legal brakes.

More common was the creation of "clone" motorcycles, as with Indian. Many original makers sold their machines either assembled or unassembled to budding entrepreneurs. These farsighted individuals might not have had the engineering know-how to design their own motorcycles, but they did have deep pockets to finance assembling, distribution, and sales of machines. Indian fought its rival—yet legal—cousins at every step. As one Indian ad read: "There may be motor

bicycles that look like the Indian, but looks are deceitful; they are not the equals of the 'Hedstrommed' Indian. . . . When you buy, buy the 'real thing'—the genuine Indian."

Indian was not completely pure, either. Premier Indian historian Jerry Hatfield believes that Hedstrom based his "original" Indian engine design on a motor created in 1901 by fellow American Emil Hafelfinger, who indeed noted in an advertisement that "Four of the leading Motorcycle Motors are copies of this Motor."

1929 HARLEY-DAVIDSON D
Harley-Davidson's new D Series arrived in 1929 powered by a 45-ci (737-cc) side-valve V-twin. Designed to do battle with Indian's famed Series 101 Scout, the Forty-Five upped the ante by using a constant-mesh transmission. Owner: Eldon Brown.

THE WRECKING CREW

In 1914, Harley-Davidson decided to go racing, and the war with Indian began in earnest. The Milwaukee factory had adamantly refused to sponsor racing throughout its first decade—although it had proudly championed in its ads race victories won by Harley-mounted privateers. Racing had become a big deal. Harley-Davidson wanted its share of the trophies—and the glory.

At the major July 4, 1914, race in Dodge City, Kansas, Harley lined up a team of six V-twins to do battle with the Indians and other marques over a 300-mile (484-km) course. The Indians quickly outpaced the Harleys, and only two of the Milwaukee machines finished—far back in the dust.

Undaunted, the Harley team continued to challenge Indian's supremacy on the racetracks throughout the year, eventually taking home the trophy for a National Championship race in Birmingham, Alabama.

In 1915, Harley was back. At the Milwaukee factory, new racing machines had been built, including a batch of F-head V-twins. During

BROADSLIDER, 1950

ABOVE: *Trev "Daredevil" Deeley slides his Harley racer with the throttle full open at an Edmonton, Alberta, contest. In 1973, Deeley's company became the distributor for Harley-Davidson in Canada, and from 1985 to 1990, he was a member of Harley's board of directors. (Photograph from City of Edmonton Archives)*

"THE SPORT OF SPORTS," 1939

LEFT: *Indian copy writers were almost besotted by the glories of their last machine in this ad, stating that the Indian Junior Scout was "an engineering triumph with peppy pickup and punchy power, easy to handle and a miracle of economy to operate."*

the year, Harley riders raced to victory in twenty-six major events as well as in countless smaller venues. Indian and Excelsior had to grudgingly sit up and take notice of the upstart. Harley's race team, nicknamed the Wrecking Crew, was duking it out with Indians, Excelsiors, Merkels, and Cyclones on board tracks and flat tracks, and at the national races sponsored by the FAM.

Over the next two decades, Indian and Harley remained gentlemen competitors on the surface. At the racetracks, however, they traded insults, raced until their engines burst, and fought tooth and nail for every trophy and every kiss from the trophy girl.

PLAYING FOLLOW-THE-LEADER

Throughout the 1920s and 1930s, the battle between Harley and Indian naturally spilled over onto the salesroom floors. This competition between the two dominant makers not only characterized the culture of American motorcycling but also shaped—for better or worse—the technical development of American motorcycles, a heritage that continues to this day.

Although Indian's and Harley-Davidson's laurels rest primarily on their V-twins, both makers began with singles and staked their reputations on one-cylinder machines for much of their first decade of production.

In 1907, Indian introduced its first V-twin, the engine still mounted in a diamond bicycle frame similar to that of its premier model. The 42-degree V-twin displaced 39 ci (650 cc), although this twin was soon followed in 1909 by a larger twin of 60.32 ci (983 cc) mounted in a loop-framed chassis.

Indian's V-twin may have been developed in response to the Curtiss V-twin of 1905. Starting in 1903, Glen Curtiss was Indian's chief threat on the racetrack, winning his share of trophies before the Indian could reach the checkered flag. Curtiss also held many a speed record that Indian coveted for its own. The G. H. Curtiss Manufacturing Company of Hammondsport, New York, offered its V-twin as a 42-ci (688-cc) F-head machine.

Harley was quick to follow the trend. The first notice of Milwaukee's prototype V-twin appeared in the *Bicycling World and Motorcycle Review* in April 1908, describing a 6-hp, 53-ci (869-cc) machine under development. In August 1908, the magazine told of a 61-ci (1,000-cc) Harley V-twin.

Harley's V-twin was first introduced as a 1909 model. The cylinders were canted at 45 degrees and measured 3.00x3.50 inches (76.2x88.9 mm) in bore and stroke, displacing 49.48 ci (811 cc). The engine was rated at 7 hp, promising a top speed of 65 mph (105 kph). Intake valves were atmospherically operated (that is, the vacuum caused when the pistons were pulled down the cylinder bores on the intake stroke "sucked" open the intake valves, whereas the exhaust valves were opened by a camshaft-operated pushrod), as on all the early Harley singles.

Harley's pride was absent from the 1910 line, only to re-appear in

In a sweep of the eye, we can see that these 1940 Harley-Davidsons are new! They are distinct, different, streamlined, and breathe the spirit of speed and power!
—Harley-Davidson advertisement, 1940

1911 as a 49.48-ci (811-cc) twin and in 1912 as a second 60.32-ci (988-cc) model, both with advanced mechanically operated inlet valves.

Sensing the tide of American motorcycling, the Reading-Standard Company of Reading, Pennsylvania, followed the trend in 1908 with an F-head V-twin. Thor was building Indian's V-twin engines under license, so it offered its own V-twin in 1909 and sold engines to the Minneapolis Motor Company of Minneapolis, Minnesota, to build its 1909 machine. Excelsior followed suit in 1910 with its 50-ci (819-cc) V-twins boasting mechanically operated inlet valves. The Merkel-Light V-twin also arrived in 1910, followed in 1912 by one from Colonel Albert Pope's Pope Manufacturing Company of Hartford, Connecticut.

The competition between Harley and Indian—as well as the rest of the smaller firms—became so intense that Springfield and Milwaukee seemed to be playing "follow the leader." When Indian deviated from the norm to launch an opposed-twin in 1917, Harley rushed its own version into production by 1919. Springfield's side-valve Model O displaced 15.7 ci (257 cc), so Milwaukee's Sport upped the ante to 35.6 ci (583 cc). At the same time Harley's machine made it to market, Indian decided to discontinue its opposed twin as the engine layout may have been too novel for the marketplace. The Harley Sport soldiered on only until 1923.

When Indian feinted, Harley flinched; when Harley bluffed, Indian blinked. When Harley increased engine displacement, Indian quickly bored out its cylinders. Indian had its Chief and Big Chief; Harley had its 61- and 74-ci (1,000- and 1,200-cc) Big Twins. Indian had its Scout; Harley had its 45-ci (750-cc) middleweight twins. Harley had its three-wheeled Servi-Car; Indian had its Dispatch Tow. Even optional equipment, accessories, and clothing items offered by each

[The Indian Scout] was the ideal machine for a head stand.
—Lucky Lee Lott

90

1939 HARLEY-DAVIDSON 61 OHV MODEL EL

The "Knucklehead" moniker came from the shape of the aluminum-alloy rocker boxes that crowned Harley-Davidson's fabulous new overhead-valve V-twin. The 61 OHV was first available as the 61-ci (988-cc) Models E and high-compression EL sportster. In 1941, Harley bowed to demand from police departments for more power and introduced the 74-ci (1,212-cc) Models F and FL. Power for this EL was a muscular 40 hp at a loping 4,800 rpm, pushing the massive 515-pound (234-kg) cycle to a top speed of 100 mph (161 kph). Owner: Eldon Brown.

company mirrored the other's. One of the few fronts on which the two did not do battle was in the four-cylinder market. Harley never offered its own four-cylinder—although it tried, experimenting with 80- and 90-ci (1,310- and 1,475-cc) V-fours in 1928. But then again, the Indian Four did not last, exiting production in 1942, long before the Harley-Indian war was over.

THE VALVETRAIN WAR

It was something as simple and basic as the placement of valves in the cylinder heads that eventually turned the tide forever in Harley-Davidson's favor and hastened Indian's demise.

In the pioneering days, most motorcycle engines featured their inlet valve mounted above the exhaust valve in a pocket set to the side of the cylinder. This engine layout was variously known as inlet-over-exhaust, pocket-valve, or F-head. The configuration tended to burn out exhaust valves, stranding many a rider by the side of a road to the derision of those who had instead bought a horse. Still, in the first decades of American motorcycling, it was the rare engine that did not feature the F-head layout.

The next development in valve configuration arrived on the Reading Standard motorcycle of 1906. Instead of having its valves placed above each other, the Reading Standard mounted them side by side on the side of the cylinder, a layout known not surprisingly as a side-valve engine. In about 1910, the Thiem Manufacturing Company of St. Paul, Minnesota, followed suit, introducing a side-valve, or flathead, single. The layout offered better performance and suffered less frequent valve failure than on the F-head, and allowed the valve gear to be safely enclosed away from the dirt and grime of the road.

Side-valves were obviously a giant step into the future, but it was not until 1916 that Indian offered a side-valve engine, launching its new Powerplus lineup. It would take Harley-Davidson another decade, making the complete changeover to side-valves as late as 1929.

Lurking in the shadows was another engine design that had been experimented with in Europe on both motorcycles and automobiles: overhead-valve engines, in which the valves are placed above the cylinder, offering dramatically improved airflow and thus more power. Unfortunately, the overhead-valve engines also ran hotter and required a much more complicated valvetrain than the crude

1941 HARLEY-DAVIDSON 45 OHV PROTOTYPE

Following the debut of its 61 OHV, Harley-Davidson toyed with topping its Forty-Five with overhead valves as well. The Forty-Five was Harley's smaller, economical model, however, and the planned 45 OHV proved prohibitively expensive. Owner: Carman Brown.

but efficient pushrod system that drove most side-valves.

Nevertheless, overhead valves were the route to more power. Indian experimented with a series of short-lived eight-valve overhead-valve racers in 1911. In 1916, Harley-Davidson ventured to build a series of eight-valve overhead-valve racers with the assistance of English engineer Harry Ricardo. Even so, with years of development in their heads, the side-valve Indians still proved their worth against the overhead-valve Harleys. After World War I, however, the tables began to turn and overhead-valve engines powered Harley's Wrecking Crew to dominate all comers.

Yet, neither Harley nor Indian offered an overhead-valve engine for the street. Tradition was certainly a roadblock, but the cost of developing a reliable overhead-valve valvetrain was also a problem. So, Harley-Davidson and Indian fans were left no choice but to remain content with their F-head and side-valve rides throughout the 1910s, 1920s, and most of the 1930s.

Some in North America saw the tide turning much earlier. Colonel Albert L. Pope offered his first V-twin in 1912 with technical innovations that were miles ahead of the Indians and Harleys of the day. The Pope Model L boasted pushrod-operated overhead valves powering its 61-ci (1,000-cc) engine to 15 hp. The Pope also rode on plunger rear suspension some three decades before most other American motorcycles had any form of rear suspension.

The same was not the case in Europe, however. The ferocious competition on the road and track pushed companies to work overtime in developing overhead-valve engines. By the dawn of the 1930s, most every major European motorcycle maker that had hopes of staying in business had overhead-valve models for sale.

By the mid-1930s, the American motorcycle industry was in trouble. Harley and Indian had battled with each other for decades, but now they were up against a more daunting foe in the form of the Great Depression, which was slowing motorcycle sales to a trickle. Harley's sales alone were cut almost in half from 1929 to 1931, and cut in third again by 1933. In addition, a handful of European motorcycles were also beginning to invade the grand old makers' turf, stealing trophies from out of the hands of the faithful and winning away some buyers with their dazzling overhead-valve machinery. A secret weapon was needed.

1943 HARLEY-DAVIDSON WLC
Harley-Davidson's W Series donned an olive drab uniform and took up the patriotic fight during World War II. Harley first built the WLC for the Canadian Army, followed by the WLA for the American and British forces. To cut costs, the WLC and WLA eschewed chrome plating and any other extras that did not serve a military purpose. The engine was Harley's stalwart W Series workhorse displacing 45 ci (737 cc) and creating 23 hp at 4,600 rpm. The weight was a massive 576 pounds (262 kg). Owners: Reg Hodgson and Jim Fitzgerald.

WINNING THE WAR

In 1931, Bill Harley began developing Harley-Davidson's future in the form of a radical new engine. Built on the foundation of a new "sump oiler" bottom end, this 61-ci (1,000-cc) motor would be crowned by an overhead valvetrain. Development would continue for five long years while the Motor Company endured the Depression and dealers begged for a new model that would give them a sales edge over their Indian rivals.

Production of the new 61 OHV (the "OHV" standing for "overhead

1947 INDIAN CHIEF

Owner Bob Shea: "The Indian Chief is deeply engraved in the memory of everyone who had the pleasure of owning or riding one. These large American motorcycles were the dream of many a young man back in the postwar years, and today these legendary machines are still setting hearts on fire. I've been restoring and riding them for years.

"So, what's it like to operate one of these iron steeds? To get my machine started, I prime the cylinders with full choke and two good kicks on the kickstarter while leaving the key off. After this, I open the choke, retard the spark a little, open the throttle a bit, and turn the key on. Then, if I hold my tongue right, she should start. After the engine has warmed up for a minute or two (it's just like an old snake: cold blooded) and her throat is clear, I bring the throttle to a closed position and retard the spark until the engine runs as slow as possible. Now I'm ready to roll. I depress the clutch pedal, engage first gear, and if nobody is watching, release the clutch, and I'm happily heading off down the road.

"The Chief is an agile machine. It has a three-speed transmission with a long-legged third gear, and easily reaches 90 mph. Fuel consumption is around 30 miles to the gallon, and it doesn't really matter which gets filled up first, the oil or the gas: It seems that on long-distance trips I'm always filling both."

1947 INDIAN CHIEF

The American motorcycling world would never be the same after the introduction of overhead valves on Harley-Davidson's 61 OHV, but the Indian faithful still stood behind their side-valve Chiefs. By 1948, the Chief's Big Twin displaced 73.62 ci (1,206 cc) and fathered 40 hp. Top speed in stock form was 85 mph (136 kph), but with special cams, polished ports, and dead-on timing, a Chief could outrun a 61 OHV Knucklehead to 105 mph (168 kph). As Indian ads boldly stated: "There's magic in the name Indian." Owner: Bob Shea.

1948 INDIAN CHIEF

The Knucklehead might have boasted overhead valves compared with the Chief's side valves, but Harley-Davidson's styling had nothing on the glorious curves and deep skirted fenders of the Indian. The Chief might have departed to its happy hunting grounds in 1953, but it lives on as one of the greatest of American motorcycles. Owner: Dave Martin.

valves") model was finally approved for 1935—and then canceled at the last minute due to further engine problems. Even after the future was unveiled to the enraptured dealers on November 25, 1935, and "Cactus" Bill Kennedy emptied his six-shooter into a chandelier in joy, it would be several long, hard months before the first production cycles were shipped to lucky dealers. Many dealers could not even get a 61 OHV until mid-1936, and these they kept as showroom samples so they could write orders and pray for future delivery.

Indian, however, saw the future in a different light. The Wigwam stood stalwart behind its tried-and-true Chief, Scout, Thirty Fifty, and Four models and made the decision not to update their flathead engines with overhead valves.

At the same time, Indian looked to the successful British vertical-twin motorcycles as inspiration. In 1945, Indian's new owner, Ralph B. Rogers, bought the Torque Engineering Company of Plainfield, Connecticut, which had created a modular engine prototype penned by former Indian engineer G. Briggs Weaver. The modular design featured overhead valves, and Indian looked down the road to producing a single, a twin, and a four. The single and twin finally entered Indian's lineup alongside the stalwart Chief and Scout in 1948, after several setbacks.

Indian was banking on its new vertical engine, but it was a bad bet. The new machines suffered numerous large and small problems, but most importantly, the dedicated Indian faithful did not take to them. In their minds, Indians were supposed to be V-twins. It would

be better to update the classic models or rekindle the grand old Four.

At almost the same time as Indian's all-American version of the British vertical twin made its debut, the true British twins invaded North America in droves. British currency had been devalued simply to increase the country's flagging exports, and Triumph, BSA, and Norton twins began to roll onto America's roads.

By the end of the 1940s, Indian was ailing. In 1950, Rogers resigned, and the British invasion that began with imported motorcycles took over Indian when a British marketing conglomerate headed by J. L. Brockhouse took control of the Wigwam.

Indian did not succumb easily, however. The great Chief soldiered on with much the same specifications until 1953, by which time Harley had developed its Panhead, a further refinement from the 61 OHV Knucklehead that sparked the revolution. Indian attempted to resurrect its V-twin heritage by joining forces with the British Vincent concern to supply its glorious engine to be mounted in Indian chassis, but the project never came to pass. After Brockhouse took over, the British firm put the Indian name on the side of Royal Enfield, Horex, Norton, and Velocette gas tanks, and imported a number of two-stroke motorcycles and mini-bikes, all in a last ditch effort to stay alive. By the mid-1950s, the company was essentially gone, living on as a marketing ploy and a label to be licensed to the highest bidder.

Today, dispute over the Indian badge continues as various entrepreneurs try to revive the lineage. The name may never be allowed to rest in peace. Meanwhile, Harley-Davidson thrives on a decision made in 1931 to build an overhead-valve version of its classic V-twin.

1947 WHIZZER H AND 1945 ZEPHYR

Two versions of motorized bicycles were revived following World War II to provide economic transportation in the postwar days. Whizzer began in 1939 with a basic clip-on bicycle powerplant before stepping up to offering complete machines with a motorized, belt-drive Schwinn bicycle. The Zephyr was powered by a Briggs & Stratton engine. Whizzer owner: Terry Frounfelker. Zephyr owner: Reynolds-Alberta Museum.

Albert G. Crocker hated Harley-Davidson. In the United States, if you weren't a Harley man, you were an Indian man, tried and true. Crocker's scorn had deep roots, stretching all the way back to the 1910s when he campaigned a Thor against Harleys in endurance races. By 1913, Crocker's loathing had become a matter of dollars and cents when he bought out the Indian dealership and regional office in Denver, Colorado. In 1914, he ran the Kansas City, Missouri, Indian branch and was competing with Harley-Davidson for checkered flags, trophy-girl kisses, and the customers' hard-earned dollars.

Crocker was not alone in hating the Motor Company. While in Kansas City, he made the acquaintance of a brazen young rider named Roland "Rollie" Free, who perhaps disliked Harley even more than did Crocker. Free had sworn vengeance on Harley since the day in the early 1920s when felt he had been cheated by a Harley dealer who presented him with an ill-prepped machine. Together, Crocker and Free made a great team.

The first thing this dynamic duo did was to start winning trophies away from Milwaukee. Then, sales of street bikes followed. Before Harley knew what was happening, Indian owned Kansas City, and a Harley enthusiast thought twice about riding into town.

In 1928, Crocker moved on and bought the Indian branch in Los Angeles, California. The story was the

same here, but now Crocker had as his sidekick a young engineering wizard named Paul Bigsby, known to everyone as "P. A." A pattern maker by trade, Bigsby had won the Big Bear Run back in his early days, and he reveled in hotting up motorcycles and custom-fabricating his own race parts. When one of Bigsby's cycling buddies, country music guitar picker Merle Travis, asked P. A. to make a solid-body electric guitar for him, Bigsby replied, "I can build anything." And it was true. Bigsby's guitar was reputed to be the inspiration for Leo Fender's revolutionary Esquire guitar, and he also designed the Bigsby guitar tailpiece that is still popular to this day. Once again, Crocker and Bigsby made a great team.

In 1931, Crocker got serious in his war with Harley-Davidson. With Bigsby at his side, Crocker crafted speedway frames that held Indian Scout 45-ci (750-cc) V-twins. He then created a conversion kit to modify the side-valve Scout engine to overhead valves. In 1933, the Crocker Motorcycle Company launched its own 30.50-ci (500-cc) single-cylinder, overhead-valve speedway racers that pumped out 40 hp.

It was in 1936 that Crocker unveiled his masterpiece, an audacious new motorcycle with a 45-degree, 61-ci (1,000-cc), overhead-valve V-twin engine, to the shock of Harley-Davidson—and probably Indian. The motorcycle boasted aluminum gas tanks and other weight-saving components, so it tipped the scales at a mere 475 pounds (216 kg) wet versus 565 pounds (257 kg) for Milwaukee's prized new Model E Knucklehead. The constant-mesh gearbox startled Indian, who still stood by their ancient sliding-gear transmissions. Most of all, however, it was 50–53 hp of the Crocker's overhead-valve engine that gave it an edge over Harley's flagship 61 OHV, which only put out about 40 hp.

The Motor Company's response was typical. Harley's Joe Petrali got hold of a Crocker and took it apart with a lawyer and photographer gazing over his shoulder to make certain no Harley parts were used or patents abused. Not surprisingly—to everyone except Milwaukee, that is—Crocker had absolutely no desire to use anything designed by Harley. With that settled, Harley then began putting the screws to parts suppliers in an attempt to make them choose Harley or Crocker, and force the latter out of business.

How much Harley hurt Crocker is hard to say from today's vantage, but the fledgling upstart had other problems to contend with as well. Crocker and his crew were custom-building every single one of the sixty or so Crocker V-twins that were eventually made. As Gene Rhyne, former Excelsior hill-climbing champ and Crocker assembler, told historian Jerry Hatfield, "I figured it out one time. It cost us $5,000 to build a machine you could buy for 550 bucks out the door."

The Crocker motorcycle came and went in a hurry. Al Crocker had created a masterpiece with his V-twin, a motorcycle that still makes hearts go aflutter, but in the end, the Motor Company won this war with one of its staunchest competitors.

1938 CROCKER
Albert G. Crocker seemingly devoted his life to battling the menace from Milwaukee. In 1936, Crocker unleashed his masterpiece, the Crocker Big Twin. With its 45-degree V-twin, the engine architecture may have mirrored Harley's, but Crocker's 61-ci (1,000-cc) punched out 50 to 53 hp—a minimum of 10 hp more than Harley's prized 61 OHV. Owner: Eldon Brown.

Chapter 6

THE
INVASION

HOW THE REST OF THE WORLD FOREVER CHANGED NORTH AMERICAN MOTORCYCLING

BRITISH INVASION, 1940S

ABOVE: *Bernie Nicholson of Saskatoon, Saskatchewan, rests on his 1948 Triumph Tiger 100 with Mount Rundle and Banff, Alberta, in the far distance. Bernie and brother Lawrence established Nicholson Brothers Motorcycles in 1934 in Saskatoon, distributing Triumph, BSA, Ariel, and Sunbeam machines.*

1949 VINCENT–HRD RAPIDE

LEFT: *Vincent's Rapide was completely built around its engine. The glorious 998-cc overhead-valve V-twin served as a stressed member of the chassis with the swing arm pivoting from the rear and the front forks attached to the top via a small backbone frame. Weighing a svelte 447 pounds (202 kg) and boasting a top speed hovering around the magical ton of 100 mph (161 kph), the Rapide and the sporting Black Shadow were everything an American motorcycle wasn't. To many, the Vincent V-twins are the quintessential motorcycle: purely functional and simply beautiful. Owner: John Oland.*

For all practical purposes, the British motorcycle invasion began on September 13, 1948. At the time, Harley-Davidson and Indian ruled the roost in the American motorcycling world as they had for decades and as they would for years more. They battled each other for the checkered flag on Sunday and then fought again on the salesroom floor on Monday. Milwaukee was currently up one notch over the Wigwam in Springfield, as it held the U.S. record for the fastest production motorcycle at 136 mph (219 kph).

All that was about to become ancient history.

A wealthy American motorcycle and car enthusiast and journalist named John Edgar had a jones for European machinery. He would go on to import one of the first race cars in the United States from a then-little-known factory called Ferrari and campaign it in West Coast road races. At the moment, however, he was lusting for a fast motorcycle, a motorcycle that could beat any Harley-Davidson or Indian.

Edgar happened to meet up with Philip Vincent, the colorful and charismatic head of the British Vincent motorcycle company, who was in California at the time recovering from a headfirst tumble onto the tarmac during a speed run on one of his finest. Always quick to extol the virtues of his fast motorcycles, Vincent promised Edgar that the American speed record would fall to his new Black Shadow model. Vincent was also then a little-known name in the United States, but listening to Vincent's words, Edgar was ready to fall under the spell.

In April 1948, Vincent cabled his chief engineer, the irascibly brilliant Phil Irving, requesting that a Black Shadow be prepped immediately and shipped to the United States.

Vincent was eager to prove his new motorcycle because his own reputation was on the line. The Black Shadow had been conceived on the sly, hidden from even the managing director of Vincent's own company, who had vetoed plans to build the machine. Irving and Vincent factory rider George Brown had secretly converted a brace of Vincent Rapides based on lessons learned from the factory's hot-rod road racer, nicknamed "Gunga Din." Inevitably, the managing director uncovered the clandestine project, and now the Black Shadow was in jeopardy.

Irving went to work. He and his crew breathed on a Series B Black Shadow destined for Edgar. Irving ground a new cam profile designed for top-end speed, and Brown went out and rode the test Black Shadow up to 143 mph (230 kph) at the local airfield before he ran out of pavement. Happy with the test, Irving had the cycle crated and shipped.

1949 VINCENT-HRD RAPIDE

Owner John P. Oland: "Power on tap for all occasions—from low-speed torque to effortless 100-mph cruising—characterizes the Vincent Rapide. I always think the relaxed low-rpm rhythm of the engine is a bit uncanny as the road rushes below me at high speed. I'm also impressed at how this motorcycle will cruise all day at well above the posted limit and, for a bonus, deliver over 50 miles to the gallon.

"Starting is deceptively easy. I tickle both carburetors, ease up on the compression, pull in the decompression lever, then give a big push on the kickstarter and release the decompression lever at the same time. I am usually rewarded with a sound that for people like me is nothing short of symphonic, but is definitely anti-social to most others.

"Most motorcycles will out-handle the Rapide on the twistees but none will cover ground in such an effortless manner. The clutch is unusually light, gear changes are sure but not to be rushed, and once in fourth gear there is flexibility from 20 to 100 mph. Braking is reassuringly effective from the twin front drums and single drum at the rear. My only wish is that the riding position for my 6-foot-4-inch height could be less cramped.

"This motorcycle always draws a crowd wherever I go and is looked upon, even by non-enthusiasts, as a work of art. When not in use, the Rapide rests in my showroom where, even after a dozen years, I never get tired of admiring its classic beauty."

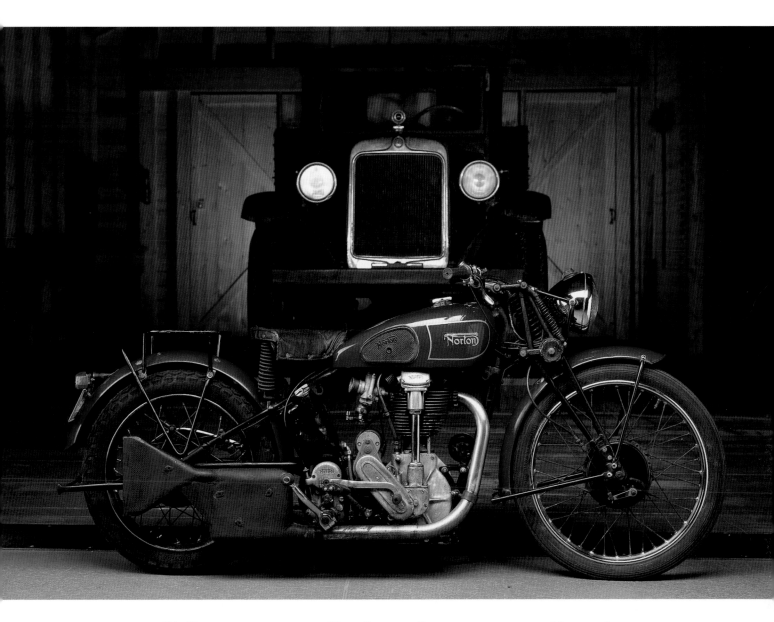

"A Gentleman of the Old School"

Now Edgar needed a rider. Enter Roland "Rollie" Free, a fearless
Harley-Davidson hater who had seemingly sworn his life to battling
the menace from Milwaukee. Free was an original. His mentor had
been O. K. Newby, the former captain of the Flying Merkel board-
track race squad. Newby later teamed with Free riding a Wall of
Death in Depression-era carnivals where a lion was turned loose in
the barrel to take swipes at the rider as he circled the top at speed. As
Free's friend Mike Parti later described him to Vincent historian
Zachary Miller: "Rollie Free was a gentleman of the old school. He'd
never swear in front of ladies, but he'd fistfight at the drop of a hat."
Free had long been an Indian devotee, using his own home-engi-
neered hot-rod Redskins to outgun Harleys on the track and in count-
less duels on the street. He had also set a handful of speed records on
Indians. Altogether, he was the perfect man for the job.

Free looked over this strange, new English motorcycle upon its

1932 Norton International

*Norton introduced its International
model in 1932 as its flagship machine
for sporting riders on the road or
amateurs and privateers on the
racetrack. Both 350-cc and 500-cc
single-cylinder versions were
available, the 500 creating 29 hp and
pushing the "Inter" to a top speed of
85 mph (137 kph). When the
International first arrived in North
America, it proved its mettle against
larger-bore Harleys and Indians V-
twins, taking home its share of race
trophies. Owner: Mark Williams.*

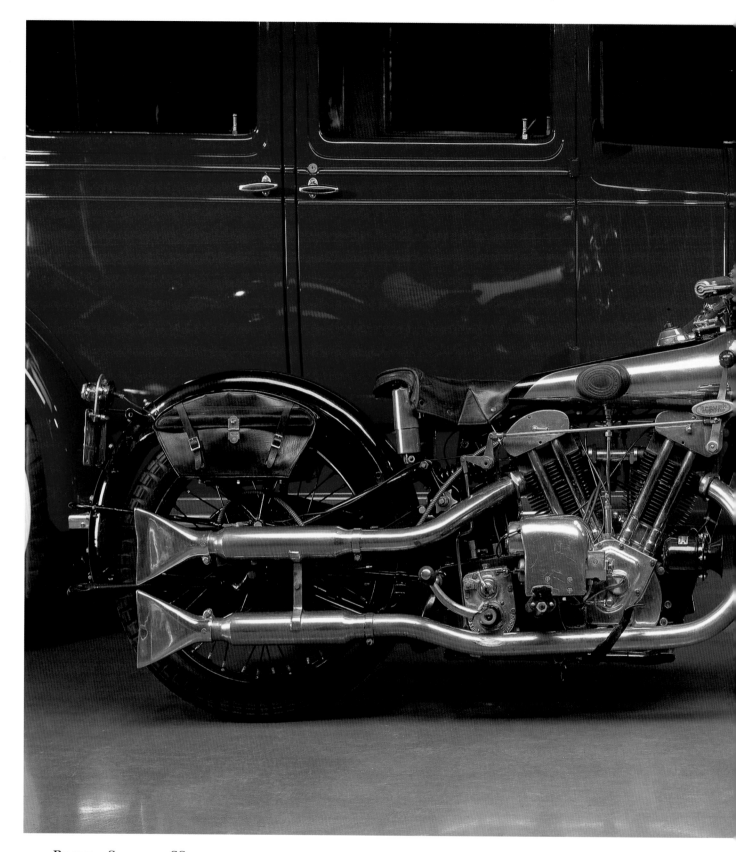

1929 BROUGH SUPERIOR SS100

George Brough's first machine was displayed in 1920 and soon earned praise as "the Rolls-Royce of motorcycles." Brough prided himself on the styling, finish, and performance of his flagship model, the Brough Superior SS100. Power came from engines sourced from JAP, Matchless, or MAG, which displaced 1,000 cc and typically creating around 45 hp. Top speed was about 100 mph (161 kph), a heady figure for its day. Owner: Peter Gagan.

1929 BROUGH SUPERIOR SS100

Owner Peter Gagan: "Every time I start my Brough, its glad roar seems to jar nearby houses, and I imagine that one of my neighbours is saying, 'There he goes again, the noisy beggar.'

"The SS100 is a top-gear machine: It runs as sweet in high as most single cylinders do in middle. I head out, chugging along White Rock Beach at the posted speed limit. Round the bend past the farm and the way straightens. The engine's docile strength waits behind one tiny lever for the pleasure of my hand. Another bend and I have the honor of one of Surrey's straightest radar-free roads. The burble of the exhaust unwinds like a long cord behind me. Soon my speed snaps it, and I hear only the cry of the wind. The cold air rushes into my dissolving eyes, so I screw them into slits and focus two hundred yards ahead on the undulating road. Like arrows, tiny bugs prick my cheeks, and sometimes a heavy housefly or beetle crashes into my skin like a well-aimed bullet.

"I pull the throttle wide open and swoop across the dips and fly up-down-up-down through the switchback beyond. The weighty machine launches itself into the air at the take-off of each rise, landing with such a snatch of the driving chain that my spine receives an unkind jolt.

"Satisfied with the fun I've just had, I give the engine two extra dollups of oil for fear that it might be running hot, but all is well. In fact, I feel confident that this machine could carry me to the moon and back."

1949 MOTO GUZZI ASTORE

Moto Guzzi of Mandello del Lario, Italy, experimented with many differing engine layouts over the years: sloper singles, vertical twins and fours, inline racing fours, V-twins in various configurations, and, of course, the famous V-8. But much of the firm's laurels rest on its horizontal singles, which debuted to power the first Guzzi of 1921 and continued until recent years in the police and military Nuovo Falcone. The Astore arrived in 1949 powered by a 498-cc horizontal single, which necessitated a long wheelbase, giving the machine graceful lines and solid handling. Owner: Roger Slater.

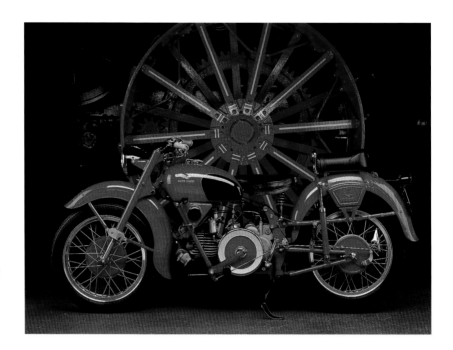

1951 ARIEL SQUARE FOUR

Edward Turner's Square Four design was a sensation when it premiered in 1930. The engine's architecture, featuring basically two parallel twins in a common crankcase, solved the problem of fitting a four into a compact motorcycle chassis. The Ariel solution resulted in a machine with four-cylinder power and smoothness. By 1951, the Square Four displaced 997 cc and put out 40 hp. Owner: Trev Deeley Motorcycle Museum.

unpacking and immediately set to work. He stripped it of all unnecessary parts, junked the front fender, and threw out the large, comfortable bench seat, replacing it with a tiny pad mounted atop the rear fender.

Because Edgar was a friend of management at Mobil Oil, the oil company offered its help, in recognition of which, twin Mobil Pegasus stickers were slapped on either side of the gas tank. (It was not disclosed until later that part of that Mobil friendship extended to mixing a special batch of alcohol fuel for the Vincent, a decidedly "non-production" fuel for beating the production cycle record.)

With the Vincent prepped, the team made its way to the Bonneville Salt Flats, Utah's dry lake bed that was the center of the world's speed record setters. Free kicked over the big V-twin, aimed it down the straight black line bisecting the flats, and rocketed away.

Free had developed his own patented riding style for top-speed runs. Once he had the cycle into top gear, he climbed from the standard sitting position to lay prone atop the rear fender in an effort to cut aerodynamic drag. He steered by watching the black line as it rolled beneath the cycle. This riding position was carefully plotted, as Mike Parti told Miller: "Rollie would get on the bike in front of a big mirror and have friends stand around and comment on how much frontal area he was making—like where to crouch, where to point his toes. He was looking for every little detail."

Now, on September 13, 1948, Free blasted down the salt in his racing leathers and pudding-basin helmet. When he returned to the start to check the clock, his best time indicated a speed of 148 mph (239 kph). He had bested Harley yet again.

Free was not happy, however. His new record

was fine, but he wanted more. There was something magical about hitting 150 mph (242 kph)—a "ton and a half," in British motorcycle slang—and Free lusted for it.

Free speculated that his leathers, which had flapped about hard enough to rip a seam, were slowing him down, so he stripped them off and replaced them with his bathing suit. Wearing a blue rubber bathing cap in place of his pudding basin and tennis sneakers instead of boots, he fired up the Vincent one more time.

Roaring down the salt laying prone on the Black Shadow in just his bathing suit, Free and the Vincent tripped the clock for a new record: 150.313 mph (241.898 kph).

The result shattered Harley-Davidson's record like a home run ball hit through a plate-glass window. It wasn't just the actual breaking of the record that did it, but the publicity that surrounded it as well. That amazing British-built Vincent motorcycle was catapulted into the American motorcyclist's consciousness with its new, brazen-but-true advertising line on its promotional material: "The World's Fastest Standard Motorcycle." A photo of Free breaking the record appeared in Life magazine, and went on to become one of the most famous motorcycle photographs ever, an example of the extremes to which those two-wheeled crazies would actually go.

John Edgar's Vincent Black Shadow was not the first British motorcycle in North America, of course. Yet, by breaking Harley's record and by appearing in Life, it established British motorcycles in the average motorcyclist's mind like nothing had before.

The British invasion had landed.

To the Dirt Born

A second challenge to the sovereignty of the American motorcycle on its own turf came from a surprising quarter, in a true story that echoed the theme of David and Goliath.

Motorcycle racing in North America was born and bred on dirt tracks. Early races were typically held at fairgrounds, where pioneering racers lined up alongside each other to await the waving of the green flag on oval horseracing tracks fashioned of compacted dirt. Other, point-to-point races were held on public roads that were closed for the day, but as most roads were unpaved in the early years of motorcycling, these too were "dirt-track" races. Racing on board tracks was an anomaly, although one of the most exciting and bloodthirsty.

Naturally, racing on dirt gave birth to a style of machine and riding tailored to its peculiarities. Roaring around a county-fair horse track on a hot Fourth of July before a cheering grandstand, riders slid their iron steeds through the oval turns with their inside foot down as support, feathering the throttle for control. American racing motorcycles eschewed brakes as being dangerous—which they certainly were at those times and those speeds. Rooster-tails of dust followed their progress, giving true meaning to the period's curse to slowpokes: "Eat my dust!"

The pinnacle of American racing became the annual events at

1954 VINCENT BLACK SHADOW
Although his name headlined the company, Philip Vincent created his flagship Black Shadow model in secret as his managing director had vetoed plans to build the machine. The Black Shadow was a tuned version of the Vincent Rapide—which was already a potent roadster. With a 998-cc overhead-valve V-twin creating 55 hp, the Shadow was capable of 125 mph (201 kph), marking it as the fastest production motorcycle of its day. Philip Vincent was vindicated. Owner: Brian Stanley.

Daytona Beach, Florida. The flat, smooth sand that stretched to the horizons was ideal for contesting speed records. With the addition of big, sweeping turns at each end and a return section run on a paved frontage road along the beach, an instant race oval was created that required guts to win the glory. In 1959, the tri-oval "superspeedway" with 33-degree banked turns was inaugurated, and the Daytona 200 became a true road race.

Other races also spoke of North American racing styles. The Big Bear Run was a hell-bent-for-leather dash across the Nevada and California deserts. The Catalina Grand Prix (GP), held on Catalina Island off the California coast, typified the American style of TT racing in mixing off-road, motocross segments with paved, road-racing sections in the fashion of the Isle of Man Tourist Trophy, or TT, from whence the name came. Class C racing grew up in the 1930s as a "run-what-ya-brung" class for production-based machines.

European GP-style racing was about as different from North American racing as a 45-ci (750-cc) Harley-Davidson KR twin was from the 29.91-ci (498.5-cc) Moto Guzzi Gambalunga single that ruled Europe in the late 1940s and early 1950s. European racing motorcycles were built low and lean with smaller-displacement engines that were tuned to extremes. Riders rode in a crouch, keeping their feet up and using a different fashion of finesse to make speed through turns.

Italian and other European racing machines had made their way into American race paddocks in ones and twos since the dawn of motorcycle competition, but in the late 1950s, the floodgates opened. The first arrivals were British machines, as they were the most closely paired to American standards. These were soon followed by Italian hardware that was often slotted into newly formed "lightweight" classes with speeds that sometimes bested the fastest Harley or Indian.

On the West Coast, a small group of European GP fans founded the American Federation of Motorcyclists (AFM), affiliated with Europe's Fédération Internationale de la Moto (FIM). The AFM held what may be the first GP-style race in the United States in April 1957 at San Gabriel, California, including entries of a privately imported Ducati 98-cc (5.9-ci) Gran Sport and two 175-cc (10.5-ci) MV Agusta racers. Classes were set up for 500- (30-ci), 350- (21-ci), 250- (15-ci), and 175-cc (10.5-ci) machines. The Canadian Motorcycle Association of the 1950s was also aligned with the FIM; it had an Unlimited Class for all displacements and a Lightweight Class for 250 cc (15 ci) and less. Throughout the rest of North America, however, racing meant feet down through the corners as riders slid through curves sideways with the throttle wide open.

Turning the Racing World on its Head
In 1958, the American racing world was turned on its head—figuratively. The historic change began, however, by turning the competition on its head—literally.

1946 BSA B31
When the bicycle market boomed in the late-1800s, Birmingham Small Arms of England began building its own cycles; when the newfangled motorcycle arrived on the scene and promised a bright future, BSA hopped on the bandwagon once again. While BSA did compete on the racetrack over the years, the firm was best known for offering solid everyday transportation. The B31 was a prime example, its roots dating back to the Val Page–designed machines of 1937. The all-iron, overhead-valve single displaced 348 cc. Owner: Brian Stanley.

In 1957, an entrepreneur named Ernest Wise began importing into the United States the wares of Moto Parilla, then one of Italy's largest motorcycle makers. The arrival of the Parillas marked the first large-scale importation of Italian cycles onto American soil.

At the top of the Parilla line was the Grand Sport, a svelte 175-cc (10.5-ci) single-cylinder machine with overhead valves actuated by a single cam mounted high on the left side of the engine. With alloy rims, low-mounted clip-on handlebars, rearset foot controls, and an anatomically formed gas tank that allowed riders to wrap their bodies around it while in a low-down, aerodynamic crouch, the Parilla was a new wave in the New World.

To add insult to injury, the Grand Sport was quick. A road test in Cycle magazine clocked 95.6 mph (154.2 kph), although a broken-in Parilla was promised to top an honest ton!

To test the bike, however, Cycle editor Bob Schanz first needed a lesson in the European GP riding style, and he explained for the neophyte reader how to tuck in and crouch down on a European racing machine. It was a lesson that all American road racers were about to learn.

Ernest Wise's Cosmopolitan Motors was learning other lessons. Wise and his workers were having trouble with the Parillas. They were high-strung, temperamental motorcycles, and the American tuners were shaking their heads over them. Wise lit upon the idea of importing an Italian mechanic to fettle the Italian bikes. After Wise cabled his request to the Parilla factory, twenty-seven-year-old Parilla racer, mechanic, and engineer Giuseppe "Joe" Rottigni was on his way.

Rottigni was not just your typical backroom boy who happened to know what to do with a screwdriver. He was that rare combination of a racer who also knew how to tune cycles, an engineer who could also ride. Rottigni had just won the 1957 Giro d'Italia, Italy's two-wheeled version of the Mille Miglia (a 1,000-mile [1,600-km] auto race), and he brought with him to the promised land of the United States his Motogiro-winning Grand Sport, a 250-cc (12.5-ci) bevel-drive bialbero (twin-camshaft) Parilla, and a crate full of special parts.

There was one problem, however. When Rottigni arrived in 1958, he spoke no English. That was a minor point, though, and he quickly organized Cosmopolitan to get its Parilla line up and running as well as spearheading the new Cosmopolitan Race Team. As one Parilla racer remembered, "Joe was the gear that drove Cosmopolitan." Rottigni aided Cosmopolitan's Parilla dealers and privateer racers, tuning race bikes, running his own Grand Sport, and winning races in Canada that brought Cosmo fame and fortune. Ernest Wise's son, Larry, began advertising the victories in Cycle and other magazines to spread the good word about Parilla, some of the first motorcycle ads in America to promote the old proverb, "Win on Sunday, sell on Monday."

It was at one of these races that Rottigni and his Parilla would turn American racing to a new light. The first race of the AMA season

1951 MATCHLESS G80CS
"Matchless in quality," the firm's slogan emphatically stated, but founder H. Collier & Sons of Plumstead, England, also focused on competition. Along with road racing, Matchless offered its G80CS, designed for off-road scrambles and motocross. The big overhead-valve 500-cc thumper cranked out bottom-end torque that made the G80CS a winner. Owner: Scona Cycle and Sports.

following Daytona was the National held on the winding racecourse run through the forests near Laconia, New Hampshire, on June 22, 1958. It was a race that changed American motorcycling.

THE CONSUMMATE ITALIAN RACER, 1957

Giuseppe "Joe" Rottigni was a factory tuner and rider for Moto Parilla of Milan, Italy. He won the prestigious 1957 Giro d'Italia, then brought his Parilla MSDS Grand Sport motorcycle to the United States later the same year to win lightweight races to advertise Parillas for importer Cosmopolitan Motors of Philadelphia, Pennsylvania. Rottigni's 175-cc Grand Sport was capable of an honest 100 mph (161 kph) and boasted handling characteristics that made it appear even quicker. Parillas were the first Italian motorcycles many North American racers saw in the flesh, and they represented a whole new school of racing that opened many eyes to the European Grand Prix world.

SHATTERING THE STATUS QUO

Before the race began, Rottigni was disqualified. On the starting grid, the judges pointed out that Rottigni's pudding-basin racing helmet was illegal. Rottigni spoke no English, so Larry Wise spoke for him. A conference ensued. After an argument with the judges, Rottigni pointed out that many of the other racers had the same type of helmet. He was allowed to start.

The helmet debate was a silly skirmish—but it told volumes about the times and environment in the U.S. racing fraternity. Word of Rottigni's prowess had gotten around, and strings were being pulled to keep him out of the race. Harley-Davidson was at the height of its campaign against foreign imports into the United States, which were challenging Harley on the racetracks and on the showroom floors. The debut of the Parilla at Laconia, along with one of Joe Berliner's first Ducati 175-cc (10.5-ci) racers, was the first time many in the American racing fraternity had ever seen an Italian motorcycle. Walter C. Davidson himself was at the race, and he certainly had powers within the AMA to defend the old ways.

That status quo was about to be shattered.

Rottigni was finally allowed to line up on the front row for the Lightweight Class IV race against Cliff Guild's 200-cc (12-ci) Triumph Cub and Hal Burton's 200-cc (12-ci) Jawa. Rottigni's 175-cc (10.5-ci) bike was obviously special. It wore low clip-on handlebars and rearset footpegs in the days when American racers used high bars and put their feet down in the turns flat-track style—whether they were racing on dirt or pavement. Curiously, Rottigni's one-piece leathers received special, awed mention in the *Motorcyclist* report.

From the drop of the flag, Rottigni set the pace—until the first turn, that is, where he was immediately knocked down. Larry Wise remembered the historic race: "[Rottigni] really introduced GP-style racing in this country. The Americans were 'flat tracking' their way around the road-race courses. They would dive far into the turns, and slow almost to a stop at the apex and downshift, all the while broadsliding with their foot down. Rottigni would downshift before entering a turn and pick a line and slow before actually entering the turn. The other riders would come along flying by him, but his engine revs were up, and he would come rocketing out of the turn, sometimes running over an outstretched foot of a broadsliding rider he was pursuing. . . .

"In the first turn he incredulously saw a rider broadsliding toward him even as his 'line' had him committed to a collision course. After the crash, as the whole pack passed him and the other rider, he started the bike and started to go. He soon passed the field and opened a lead followed closely only by Cliff Guild on the factory Triumph. After halfway he crashed again on an oil slick at the bottom of Laconia Hill, and the whole pack passed him again. He straightened the bent levers and pedals even though his hands were torn and bleeding. This was in front of the main crowd of spectators and they were wildly cheering for him now. At the finish line he had caught most of the riders except for two and finished third with blood streaming from his torn hands, covering the machine."

The winner of the race was Guild with Burton second. Nevertheless, the true winner was Rottigni. As Motorcyclist recounted Rottigni's feat: "It was quite apparent that he was the fastest man in the field, as well as the most seasoned. . . . Had the race gone a few more laps it would have been interesting to see if Rottigni could have again captured the winning position." In trying to catch the leaders, Rottigni had set a lap record for the 250-cc (15-ci) class on his 175-cc (10.5-ci) bike.

After the checkered flag had been waved, even Walter Davidson came forth to shake Rottigni's bloody hand.

"You Meet the Nicest People on a Honda"

At the dawn of the 1960s, a surprise attack on the world's motorcycle market came from a quarter few people could ever have guessed.

This new invasion struck North American shores first, orchestrated by Jack McCormack, who would go down in history as one of the most influential figures in American motorcycling since the early pioneers such as George Hendee, Oscar Hedstrom, Bill Harley, and the Davidson brothers.

McCormack was a former salesman for Johnson Motors of Los Angeles, the Western states Triumph distributor. By 1959, he had left JoMo to sell buttons for his father's firm, but he still made his sales calls on a 650-cc (39-ci) Triumph TR6, his business suit ruffled by the breeze.

VESPA CHIC, 1951
Enrico Piaggio's Vespa was crafted by helicopter engineer Corradino d'Ascanio, who brought advanced aviation principles to scooter design and developed the most long-lived and loved of all motorscooters. The Vespa was not the first scooter, but it was the best—and proved that with motorscooters, beauty is more than just skin deep. This image of a Vespa in Paris comes from one of Piaggio's famous promotional calendars.

1965 HONDA CUB 90

ABOVE: *"You meet the nicest people on a Honda" was the brilliant advertising jingle used to promote the strange little Hondas in the United States. At a time when motorcycling's public image was as black as used motor oil, Honda fought valiantly to redefine John Doe's perception. How bad could a machine this cute be, anyway? Introduced in 1958, the Cub is still being built today in eleven countries with more than 30 million produced—and counting. Owner: Byron Reynolds.*

1963 HONDA BENLY CB92R

RIGHT: *The CB92 Benly was a radical and potent 124-cc Honda that raised eyebrows when it was imported into North America. With its pressed-steel frame and forks, overhead-cam twin-cylinder engine, and top speed of 70 mph (113 kph), the Benly was a hot performer. A race kit was also available, and many Benlys saw action in lightweight classes. Owner: John McEwen.*

McCormack simply loved motorcycles. He was not a Marlon Brando clone in a black leather jacket. McCormack sported an all-American crew cut and looked like Mom and Dad's dream prom date for their sweet-sixteen daughter. He rode motorcycles, though, and that was enough to draw dirty looks as he rode down Main Street.

McCormack had heard word of the new Honda motorcycles that were just starting to be imported from Japan. These were different machines from the Triumph and other Brit bikes that he knew so well. The Honda cycles piqued his interest.

Following World War II, Soichiro Honda had adapted his mechanical expertise as an aftermarket maker of pistons and rings and built an empire crafting motorcycles and automobiles. He first used 50- (3-ci) and 100-cc (6-ci) gasoline generator motors from World War II aircraft to power bicycles. He next formed the Honda Motor Company in Hammamatsu to build his Model A, a motorized bicycle.

But Honda had a dream. His goal was to build a true motorcycle that would rival the best of the British machines. After a succession of clip-on engines and diminutive motorcycles, he jumped in 1955 to building the luxurious, 250-cc (15-ci) overhead-camshaft Model D, which he nicknamed the Dream. This machine signaled a technical leap that brought Honda up to date with—if not surpassing—many makers of the day.

By 1955, Honda boasted a gigantic factory complex that cranked out some 500,000 machines annually. Motorcycles bearing Honda's name were sold throughout Asia, and the firm was expanding its market into Australia, Africa, the Middle East, and Europe. In Canada, Trevor Deeley of Alberta had started importing the odd little machines earlier in 1958. Honda was the largest motorcycle maker in the world—and most Americans had never even heard the name. All of that was about to change.

THE PROMISED LAND

In 1959, Honda entered the promised land, the U.S. market. The beachhead was a nondescript storefront at 4077 Pico Boulevard in Los Angeles, California, where the American Honda Motor Company was trying to figure out how to sell its nifty Honda 50, the Cub, to the American public.

Enter Jack McCormack, who talked his way into the job of national sales manager for Honda in 1960 with dreams of popularizing motorcycling in an anti-motorcycle world. McCormack was one of several Americans to be hired by the foundling importation business, whose Japanese managers spoke only halting English; others included former racer George "Frenchy" French, Bob Hanson, Don Graves, and Doug Moncrief. McCormack outfitted each of his small crew of salesmen with a Chevrolet El Camino, the half-car, half-pickup-truck vehicle that could carry up to six Super Cubs. The "El Camino Brigade," as they were known, set out across the West to sign up dealers.

1964 HONDA CB77 SUPER HAWK

Soichiro Honda got his start in motorcycles by bolting war-surplus engines into bicycles for the war-ravaged Japanese, who were in need of inexpensive transportation. The Super Hawk established Honda's reputation in North America: The CB77 proved that the Japanese firm was capable of building solid, serious motorcycles and not just inexpensive commuter machines and teenager toys. Basically a bored-out 250, the twin-cylinder CB77 displaced 305 cc and put out 27 hp. Owner: Byron Reynolds.

1969 HONDA CB750 FOUR

Honda rewrote the standards for motorcycles when it introduced its CB750 Four in 1969. The new Honda was everything other motorcycles strove to be. It boasted disc brakes that actually braked, electrics that actually turned things on and off, and engine cases that actually kept oil inside. The 736-cc inline four featured an overhead camshaft, four carburetors, a five-speed gearbox, and an "electric leg" in the form of a starter. With 67 hp on tap, the CB750 was good for 125 mph (200 kph). The new Honda made converts of many former Triumph or Harley owners and sent motorcycle designers everywhere scurrying back to their drawing boards. Owner: Glenn Turple.

1969 Honda CB750

Owner Glenn Turple: "I rode a variety of British machines between 1946 and 1966, then suddenly found myself owning a Honda CB450. After putting 45,000 miles on it, I became intrigued by Honda's new large-displacement, four-cylinder machines when they were introduced in 1969. I quickly convinced myself to get one.

"Shortly after taking delivery of an early production CB750 (with sandcast cases), I made a ten-day return trip from Red Deer, Alberta, to San Diego, California. Over the next few years, I did a lot of touring, including one year when I really got wound up and rode 25,000 miles. In less than six years, the odometer reached 99,999 miles. But instead of letting the odometer flip over to zero, I disconnected it and mounted a CL350 speedo above the original gauges. While I kept using the 750 for cruising around town, a first-year Gold Wing became my new touring machine.

"The 750 was always a great performer and easy on maintenance. It wasn't until 1995 that I felt compelled to open up the engine for the first time. Good news! All I had to do was replace one bad valve and install a set of standard pistons.

"Almost three decades after I bought my 750, I still take it for a few spins each year, perhaps as much for my sake as the bike's. We seem to be inseparable, like good old friends who have shared lots of happy memories, though I must admit we shared some less pleasant ones too, such as the night my front wheel clipped a porcupine that was crossing the road. Hitting the critter scared the heck out of me, but the next morning I felt strangely smug as I plucked souvenir quills from my tire, right-side footrest, and leather boot. Poor porky! Then there was the time I was riding the 750 from Vancouver to Sacramento to Reno, when I encountered every miserable condition mother nature could throw at me: bitter cold temperatures, wind, rain, fog, snow, slush, and ice. Not fun stuff for biking, but I guess I should have known better—it was February!

"Until I began riding Gold Wings, I had never owned a better long-distance motorcycle than the 750. It always coaxed me to go further and always delivered me back home. For sure, it was the 750 that infected me with the touring bug. When I add up all the trips over fifty-some years, my motorcycles have taken me about 685,000 miles—and I'm not done yet!"

*Said young James, In
my opinion,
There's nothing in this world
Beats a '52 Vincent and a
red-headed girl.
Now Nortons and Indians and
Greeves won't do
They don't have a soul like a
Vincent '52*
— Richard Thompson,
"1952 Vincent Black Lightning"

Knowing firsthand that motorcycling had a bum rap, McCormack first avoided referring to the Honda motorcycles as motorcycles. "We did everything we could to keep from calling the Honda 50 a motorcycle," he told motorcycle historian Phil Schilling. "We called it a two-wheeled compact, a family fun vehicle—anything but a motorcycle. We stayed away from talking about performance or about anything other than fun."

That was all a part of his strategy of selling a motorcycle to people who hated motorcycles. McCormack also knew that he could not sell the Super Cub as transportation in the United States; he envisioned the buyers of his wares as the all-American family looking for a fun runabout.

McCormack and Honda also had another image problem to overcome. Japan was still the bad guy of World War II in America's eyes, and many Americans simply would not buy Japanese products. To others, "Made in Japan" meant *poorly* made. The sole other Japanese motorcycle line then being sold in any numbers in the United States was foisted surreptitiously on unknowing buyers. Throughout the late 1950s, Montgomery Ward sold mail-order motorscooters with the glamorous model names of the Nassau, Waikiki, and the Miami. Beneath the Monkey Ward nameplate, however, these were Mitsubishi C-74 Silver Pigeon scooters, proudly made in Japan by the former builder of the infamous Zero fighter plane of World War II.

The El Camino Brigade set up Honda franchises anywhere and everywhere they could. Some Old School motorcycle dealers signed on the dotted line to sell the new machines, such as Floyd Dreyer of California, who went on to become the operator of the oldest U.S. Honda dealership. Other Super Cubs were sold through unlikely venues such as farsighted automobile dealerships, hardware stores, even men's clothing outlets and barbershops. McCormack established 125 "dealers" in the West before pointing his El Caminos east.

Then, McCormack had a further vision: He wanted big money from Honda to spark an advertising campaign to bring Honda's "nonmotorcycle" in front of all of America. Honda accordingly upped his promotional budget from a mere $20,000 in 1960 to an astonishing $150,000 in 1961. McCormack put the money to work, running full-page ads in *Life* magazine at $40,000 a pop.

In 1962, McCormack and his crew had a brainstorm that came in the form of a marketeer's dream—the perfect advertising slogan. Someone at American Honda came upon the rallying cry, "You meet the nicest people on a Honda." With help from the firm of Grey Advertising of Beverly Hills, the ads began appearing in magazines everywhere, from *Cycle* to the *Saturday Evening Post*.

With a simple slogan, McCormack's sales force removed the stigma that a switchblade was the chief tool you needed to ride a motorcycle. Suddenly, from out of the days of *The Wild One*, the motorcycle's image got a haircut, shave, and a new set of respectable clothes. Almost overnight, the name "Honda" became nearly synony-

1967 BMW R50/2

The R50/2 was built on pure BMW tradition. From the smooth-running flat twin engine to the no-nonsense black-and-white paint scheme, the R50/2 showed its heritage, stretching all of the way back to the first BMW, the single-cylinder R32. BMW /2s proved ideal for North America: They could roll down the highway mile after mile from sea to shining sea and always provide comfort and reliability for their owners. It's little wonder that an R50/2 became one of the heroes of Robert Pirsig's seminal 1970s book, Zen and the Art of Motorcycle Maintenance. *Owner: Reinhold Borowski.*

1970 NORTON COMMANDO S

Few motorcycles boast such faithful followers as the Norton Commando. Even today, more than two decades after the last Commando rolled off Norton's assembly lines, Commandos are still spoken of with reverence. Debuting in 1968, the Commando evolved through a plethora of models. The S featured high pipes mounted to the 745-cc Atlas parallel twin-cylinder engine and 56 hp. Owner: Harry Pytel.

1972 KAWASAKI H2

Kawasaki rarely bothered making simple transportation; instead, the Japanese firm focused purely on performance. The H2 was typical Kawasaki, with more guts than the frame, forks, or brakes could handle. Before riders could catch their breath, 80 mph (128 kph) appeared on the speedometer as the two-stroke engine wound itself up. Owner: Malcolm Robertson.

mous with "motorcycle"—or at least synonymous with good, clean, crew-cut motorcycling fun.

Still, few of the Old School of real motorcyclists ever thought Honda would sell many of its oddball little machines. McCormack, nevertheless, had lofty goals—and confidence. When one Honda salesman was asked—rather snidely, of course—by a Triumph dealer how many Hondas he thought could actually be sold in the United States, the Honda rep responded, "5,000." This confidence bordered on the audacious if not arrogant to the Triumph dealer, who was fighting tooth and nail to sell 2,500 Triumphs annually in the West. Then the Honda salesman clarified his statement: "Five thousand per month!"

As with the early Volkswagen Beetles in the United States, Honda dealers began selling motorcycles like grocery stores sold milk. In 1959, American Honda sold some 2,500 machines; in 1961, it sold 17,000. By 1962, Honda was selling more motorcycles on Harley-Davidson's home turf than the Milwaukee company itself. In fact, Honda was selling more machines in the United States than were all of the rest of the industry combined. In 1963, Honda sold an amazing 90,000 of the 150,000 motorcycles sold in the United States. Not only did Honda now control 60 percent of the market, but it also had almost single-handedly tripled the size of the total market.

McCormack's El Camino Brigade had done good.

THE RIGHT PLACE

Honda was in the right place at the right time. It entered the United States just as the recreational market was set to open wide with Baby Boomers reaching driving age and the country flush with leisure time and the cash to enjoy it. Honda also helped to make the market, bringing inexpensive, reliable, easy-to-use little motorcycles that were the perfect toy. First-time motorcycle buyers made up 65 percent of Honda's customers, just as McCormack had envisioned. Most of those buyers were between sixteen and twenty-six years old—and 10 percent were female. The statistics were startling.

Some Old School motorcycle dealers of the day grudgingly approved of Honda's success. After all, the overall market was expanding as people bought Honda Super Cubs, then moved up to a 250-cc (15-ci) Honda CB72 Hawk or a 305-cc (18.3-ci) Honda CB77 Super Hawk. Some day, the dealers reasoned, these people would want a real motorcycle, and they would come calling. The Old School dealers would have their Triumphs, Nortons, and Harleys polished, gassed, and waiting.

When that day came, however, Honda unveiled a "real" motorcycle of its own. The four-cylinder CB750 of 1969 boasted power and performance, brakes that actually braked, electrics that truly turned things on and off, and engine casings that kept the oil inside the engine. In a few short years, Honda's CB750 rewrote the rules.

FAITHFUL VÉLOSOLEX RIDER, 1993

The Vélosolex was advertised as "the bicycle that runs by itself." First introduced by the French Solex firm in 1946, the Vélosolex was propelled by a 49-cc two-stroke engine mounted above the front wheel with drive directly onto the tire. A lever lowered and raised the engine, providing a simple "clutch" action. This faithful Vélosolex rider paused for photographer John Dean's camera in the streets of Auxonne, France.

NOW **FOR THE FII**
YOU CAI

COLUMBIA PICTURES
Presents
A STANLEY KRAMER
PRODUCTION

MARLON B

THE WILD

with **MARY MURPHY · ROBERT KEITH**
and **LEE MARVIN**
Screenplay by JOHN PAXTON
Directed by LASLO BENEDEK

Chapter 7

THE
WILD ONES

THE ROOTS OF THE OUTLAW
BIKER MYSTIQUE

1952 HARLEY-DAVIDSON K

ABOVE: *With British overhead-valve twins invading North American shores in droves in the post–World War II years, Harley-Davidson was running scared. Its response was marketing genius: Harley recast its old Forty-Five as a new sporting model, badged as the K Series. The engine was still the hard-working 45-ci (737-cc) side-valve V-twin, but a new four-speed gearbox with right-foot shifting and a handlever-operated clutch differentiated it from the old Forty-Fives and made it seem a worthy competitor to the Triumphs and BSAs. Weight was down to a relatively trim 400 pounds (181 kg) and top speed was 85 mph (136 kph). It took some time for the K series to catch on, but its legacy still rides the roads today as the Sportster. Owner: Carman Brown.*

THE WILD ONE POSTER

LEFT: *These days, The Wild One is considered a classic, but when it was first released in 1953, it was a box office flop. Few folk wanted to see a film about motorcycle gangs—especially one where the "bad" guy was actually kind of a good guy, an anti-hero. In the days of westerns and war movies where the good guys wore white and the bad guys were in black, a black-leather-jacketed good guy seemed all wrong.*

ST TIME
SEE

RANDO as

ONE

X

It was a day that would live in infamy. Pearl Harbor was history and World War II was finally finished, but in the days after the war, some young men returning from battle had a craving for something different from the ordered life and the American dream that they had fought for. Kickstarting a motorcycle into life and riding off to chase the horizon filled the bill. It was just such a ride that brought a group of motorcyclists searching for fun to the sleepy little town of Hollister, California, on the Fourth of July in 1947.

Motorcycling's reputation had not been sterling from day one. The infernal machines backfired and sent scared horses running wild; other footbound citizens saw cycles as a sign the times were changing and so didn't like them on principle.

Then, on September 8, 1912, Indian's star rider, Eddie Hasha, crashed while racing at the motordrome at Vailsburg Park in Newark, New Jersey. He careened up the board track and into the stands, killing himself and six spectators. The public was aghast and outraged: The Newark crash became infamous as the turning point in the downfall of the bloodthirsty sport of motordrome racing. Following Hasha's crash, all motorcycle racing lived under a black cloud for decades.

During the 1930s, motorcycle technology developed and cycles could run faster than ever, a fact that in itself scared Ma and Pa—even while Junior kneeled down almost in prayer to check out the engine. Automobiles became the standard for transportation, while motorcycles lost much of the pioneering prestige they might have held, becoming a hobbyist's toy or a racer's folly. In short, motorcycles had already become an outsider's ride.

Still, nothing compared to the outsider image heaped on motorcycling after Hollister.

What really happened at Hollister is impossible to tell. There are many versions of the story of the day that changed motorcycling forever, and none of them are consistent with each another. There's one thing they all agree on, however: The story as presented in *Life* magazine and Marlon Brando's famous—or infamous—movie, *The Wild One*, was a hoax.

THE PHOTOGRAPH

It all began with a photograph. Late editions of the San Francisco *Chronicle* on July 5, 1947, carried the first version of the story: A gang of drunken motorcyclists called the Boozefighters had invaded the town of Hollister on America's most sacrosanct day, July 4. They had raced through the streets on their motorized steeds, terrifying good people. They drank beer and brawled and distressed young damsels. Life in Hollister would never be the same.

A single photograph was sent out over the wires to news media around the country. In the photograph taken by Barney Petersen, a fat slob of a motorcyclist sat astride his Harley, surrounded by a sea of empty bottles. He clutched a couple beers in his evil hands and leered

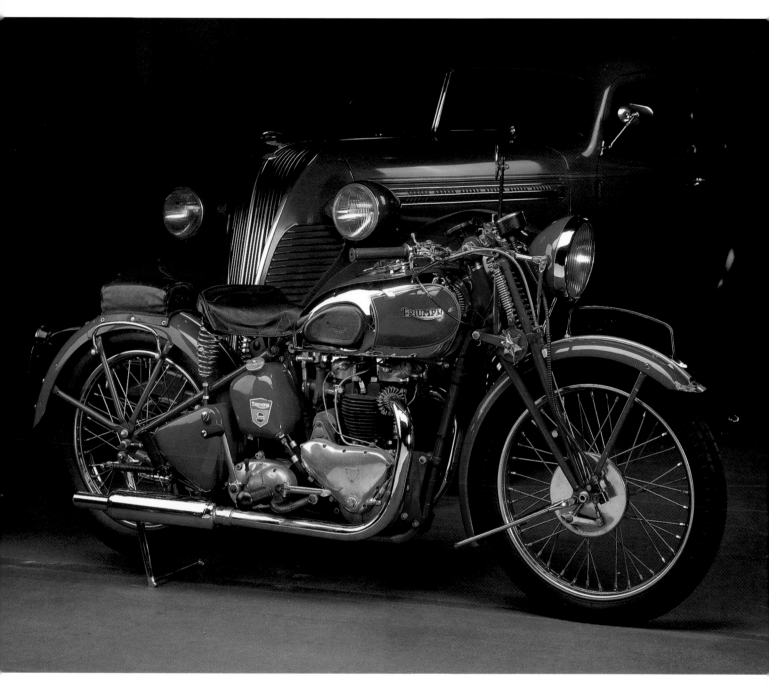

1939 TRIUMPH SPEED TWIN

Triumph chief designer Edward Turner's new Speed Twin was launched in 1937 and set the style for Triumph vertical twins for the next five decades. The Speed Twin was powered by a 498-cc vertical parallel twin that created 27 hp at 6,300 rpm, carrying the stylish machine to a top speed of 93 mph (150 kph). Owner: Trev Deeley Motorcycle Museum.

at the camera. In his eyes was a cold message: "Bar your doors and lock away your daughters because I'm coming to get you."

A photo editor at *Life* saw the photograph and marked it for use. At the time, *Life* held the respect of Americans like no magazine before or since. *Life* had told the awful story of World War II in words and photographs like Grandpa sitting down to spin a yarn in front of the fireplace after a turkey dinner with all the dressings. It was not until Walter Cronkite arrived in American living rooms every evening on the television that the news media had a more powerful single voice.

Life reported: "On the Fourth of July weekend, 4,000 members of a motorcycle club roared into Hollister, California, for a three-day convention. They quickly tired of ordinary motorcycle thrills and turned to more exciting stunts. Racing their vehicles down the main streets and through traffic lights, they rammed into restaurants and bars, breaking furniture and mirrors . . . police arrested many . . . but could not restore order."

When *Life* ran the photo with the story of the Hollister brouhaha, the awful event was catapulted into the hearts and minds of Americans everywhere. The story of Hollister had all the makings of myth. It was the modern western, with the lawless men in black riding into town to confront the good citizenry, only to be banished by a duel with the fearless lawman. It was like a war movie, a blitzkrieg by minions of the evil empire upon the peace-loving townspeople. Almost overnight, a new menace was at hand, and every motorcyclist was suddenly seen as one of the dreaded Boozefighters.

JOHNNY
With the stolen race trophy tied to the headlight nacelle of his trusty Triumph Thunderbird, Marlon Brando was the perfect Johnny.

THE MOVIE

Then came the movie. In 1953, *The Wild One* starring Marlon Brando opened at a theater near you. Producer Stanley Kramer and director Laslo Benedek knew a good story when they saw one. They jumped on the Hollister incident, read the news accounts, shook their heads once more at the photograph, and fashioned a fictionalized account of the event. Their film began with a warning that bore echoes of the first lines of Dante's guided tour of Hell: "This is a shocking story. It could never take place in most American towns—but it did in this one. It is a public challenge not to let it happen again."

In the film, Marlon Brando played the leader of the Black Rebels Motorcycle Club, a cool cat named Johnny Strabler who wore a black leather jacket like a suit of armor against the world. Atop his Triumph Thunderbird, he led his gang on a Fourth of July ride up the California coast, stopping to wreak havoc at a motorcycle race before moving on to terrorize an innocent small town based on Hollister.

The opening scene of the movie provides a quick Hollywood-style sociological analysis of the roots of postwar disaffection that gave birth to motorcycle gangs. A highway patrolman who had just chased away Brando's gang warns another officer.

"Where'd that bunch come from?" an officer asks, playing the devil's advocate for a theater full of moviegoers asking themselves the same question.

"I don't know," responds the other patrolman, the voice of all-knowing wisdom. "Everywhere. I don't even think they know where they're going. Nutty. Ten guys like that gives people the idea everybody that drives a motorcycle is crazy. What are they trying to prove?"

"Beats me," answers the first officer, the voice of the common people. "Looking for somebody to push them around so they can get sore and show how tough they are."

When the gang arrives in town, it makes a beeline for Bleeker's Cafe and Bar. Members drop their change into the jukebox and order up rounds of beer. One townsgirl, taken by the excitement that follows the gang, says, "Black Rebels Motorcycle Club, that's cute! Hey Johnny, what are you rebelling against?"

With studied nonchalance, Johnny answered, "Whaddya got?"

He further explained his philosophy of life to the waitress named Cathy, played by Mary Murphy. She is curious about Johnny and his gang, and queries him: "Where are you going when you leave here? Don't you know?"

Johnny: "We're just gonna go."

Cathy: "Just trying to make conversation; it means nothing to me."

Johnny: "Look, on weekends, we go out and have a ball."

Cathy: "What do you do? I mean, do you just ride around, or do you go on some sort of picnic or something?"

Johnny: "A picnic? Man, you are too square; I have to straighten you out. Now listen, you don't go any one special place, that's cornball style. You just go!" he says to a snap of his fingers. "A bunch gets together after a week. It builds up. The idea is to have a ball. Now, if you gonna stay cool you gotta wail. You gotta put something down. You gotta make some jive, don't you know what I'm talking about?"

Obviously, she doesn't have a clue.

Soon, Johnny will take Cathy for a ride on his Triumph, giving society a taste of freedom on two wheels. "I've never ridden on a motorcycle before," Cathy exclaims with delight. "It's fast. It scared me. But I forgot everything. It felt good."

Then, the true bad guy shows his face. Lee Marvin and his gang of bad bad guys ride into town. As Cathy walks home from work, Marvin on his Harley-Davidson leads his gang to encircle the woman, spinning around in a kaleidoscope of revving bikes—the Indians circling the wagon train in the Wild West—moving in for the kill. Only Johnny can save her, whisking her away on his Triumph like a knight in shining armor.

Wild and wicked . . . living with no tomorrow!
—Ad slogan for the movie
Motorcycle Gang, 1957

———

Hard riders! Mounted on burning steel! . . . with only their leathers between them and Hell!
—Ad slogan for the movie
The Sidehackers, 1969

"BUILT IN THE LIGHT OF EXPERIENCE," 1950

ABOVE: *The advertising slogan read true, as the Norton Dominator had an engine designed with the faults of the Triumph twin in mind and a Featherbed frame based on years of racing.*

1953 NORTON DOMINATOR 88

RIGHT: *Designer Bert Hopwood came to Norton in 1947 after working at archrival Triumph. His first task was to design a twin, so Hopwood sought to build a better mousetrap, drawing on lessons learned from the Triumph vertical twin. The new Norton Dominator was launched in 1948 with Hopwood's 497-cc parallel twin. In 1952, the "Domi" was substantially upgraded when Hopwood's engine was fitted into Norton's famed Featherbed and christened the 88. Owner: Murray Neibel.*

THE ANTI-HERO

Brando's character was confusing to 1950s audiences. He was the bad guy and the good guy at the same time. This didn't make sense: Everyone knew full well that the bad guys wore black hats and the good guys wore white. It was repeated every Saturday matinee in the horse opera at the local theater.

Now, suddenly, here was Johnny wearing a black leather jacket and a black cap, terrorizing a town with his good-for-nothing bikers—and then midway through the movie another side of his character gradually comes to light. Johnny ain't all bad, just confused. Under the mask of that emotionless face and the armor of his jacket, he's introspective, questioning, maybe as confused about his direction in life as the audience is confused about his character. Johnny was the first anti-hero role in Hollywood.

Marlon Brando had the look down pat. "The part was actor-proof," he wrote forty years later in his autobiography, *Songs My Mother Taught Me*. That may have been a self-deprecating brag, or perhaps Brando didn't realize that in many ways he *was* Johnny.

Brando provided his own psychoanalysis of Johnny: "More than most parts I've played in the movies or onstage, I related to Johnny, and because of this, I believe I played him as more sensitive and sympathetic than the script envisioned. There's a line in the picture where he snarls, 'Nobody tells *me* what to do.' That's exactly how I've felt all my life. Like Johnny, I have always resented authority. I have been constantly discomfited by people telling me what to do, and have always thought that Johnny took refuge in his lifestyle because he was wounded—that he'd had little love as a kid and was trying to survive the emotional insecurity that his childhood had forced him to carry into adulthood. Because of the emotional pain of feeling like a nobody, he became arrogant and adopted a pose of indifference to criticism. He did everything to appear strong when inside he was soft and vulnerable and fought hard to conceal it. He had lost faith in the fabric of society and had made his own world. He was a rebel, but a strong part of him was sensitive and tender. At the time I told a reporter that 'I wanted to show that gentleness and tolerance is the only way to dissipate the forces of social destruction' because I view Johnny as a man torn by an inner struggle beyond his capacity to express it. He had been so disappointed in life that it was difficult for him to express love, but beneath his hostility lay a desperate yearning and desire to feel love because he'd had so little of it. I could have just as easily been describing myself. It seemed perfectly natural for me to play this role."

The movie was not a hit when it made its debut. Many theater-owners refused to screen such trash; others who dared to were read the riot act by do-gooders. "The public's reaction to *The Wild One* was, I believe, a product of its time and circumstances," Brando wrote. "It was only seventy-nine minutes long, short by modern standards, and it looks dated and corny now; I don't think it has aged well. But it became a kind of cult film."

1954 HARLEY-DAVIDSON FL

ABOVE: *Harley-Davidson's Big Twin models of the 1950s and 1960s were true Cadillacs for the working class. Adorned with glowing paint schemes, dressed up by saddle bags and a luxurious seat, and jeweled with chrome, the 74-ci (1,212-cc) FL was the epitome of American motorcycling for its day. Elvis Presley owned one, and you couldn't ask for a better endorsement than that. Owner: Ben Yarschenko.*

ELVIS

LEFT: *The King sat astride a Harley-Davidson Big Twin like he was perched on his throne. As soon as Elvis Presley's first records went gold, he bought a Harley—and continued to order the latest and greatest from Milwaukee almost annually. The King never skimped on accessories, either.*

1957 BSA GOLD STAR CLUBMAN DBD34

BSA's Gold Star was the ultimate Rocker bike. In the glory days of England's Ace Café or when the Rockers feuded with the Lambretta-riding Mods at Brighton Beach, the "Goldie" was the ride. Its 499-cc thumper engine cranked out 40 hp at 7,000 rpm to carry the Clubman model to a quick ton (161 kph). Owner: John Bennett.

1957 BSA GOLD STAR CLUBMAN

Owner John Bennett: "The DBD 34 500-cc Gold Star Clubman was the last of the sporting road singles produced by BSA. Its enviable success in trials, motocross, and road racing made the Gold Star the sporting rider's choice.

"Starting a high-compression, highly tuned thumper requires a bit of talent and a lot of leg muscle. This bike does not tolerate the timid. It requires full retard on the manual competition magneto, a tickle of the Amal Grand Prix carburetor, and a determined kick to launch the engine into action. If one is not attentive when starting it, the kick lever will attempt to send the prospective rider over the handlebars.

"Operating the Clubman requires attention to the throttle. The carburetor has no idle circuit, therefore one must 'blip' the throttle to keep the engine ticking over. The tall first gear in the four-speed, close-ratio gearbox requires some clutch slippage to get underway. Around town, it would be charitable to say it lunges. But on an open, twisty road, the transformation from quirky anachronism to kinetic art-form is a revelation. Above 30 mph, the Clubman is certainly a capable performer. Its power, chassis, and brakes encourage aggressive riding. The intake honk, engine clatter, and mellow exhaust note—especially the twitter on overrun—will charm any rider with a pulse.

"I've never gotten off this bike and walked away without turning around to admire its graceful lines. Today, the Gold Star is not only an elegant classic but still a wonderfully exciting motorcycle."

The film struck a chord with a certain disaffected crowd that were tantalized by the rebellion—and by Brando's character. He was a romanticized Robin Hood on a cycle, offering would-be rebels an image to live up to. Sales of black leather jackets soared, Brando related in his autobiography, and suddenly became a symbol, although what the symbol stood for was not truly understood. It was the dawn of the juvenile delinquent craze, a horror mirrored in numerous paperback potboiler novels and Hollywood films. A new star was born riding on the wave of this craze, a young actor named James Dean, who in his film *A Rebel Without a Cause* came to stand against everything society stood for.

Brando writes that he never expected *The Wild One* to have such an impact: "I was as surprised as anyone when T-shirts, jeans and leather jackets suddenly became symbols of rebellion. In the film there was a scene in which somebody asked my character, Johnny, what I was rebelling against, and I answered, 'Whaddya got?' But none of us involved in the picture ever imagined it would instigate or encourage youthful rebellion. . . .

"After *The Wild One* was finished, I couldn't look at it for weeks; when I did, I didn't like it because I thought it was too violent."

Reading between the lines of Brando's autobiography, it seems obvious that *The Wild One* also played an important role in changing Brando's life, whether he realized it or not.

"I never knew that there were sleeping desires and feelings in our society whose buttons would be hit so uncannily in that film. In hindsight, I think people responded to the movie because of the budding social and cultural currents that a few years later exploded volcanically on college campuses and the streets of America. Right or wrong, we were at the beginning of a new era after several years of transition following World War II; young people were beginning to doubt and question their elders and to challenge their values, morals and the established institutions of authority. There was a wisp of steam just beneath the surface when we made that picture. Young people looking for a reason—any reason—to rebel. I simply happened to be at the right place at the right time in the right part—and I also had the appropriate state of mind for the role."

Je n'ai pas besoin personne au Harley-Davidson.
—Brigitte Bardot,
"Harley-Davidson"

THE REAL BOOZEFIGHTER SPEAKS

John Cameron was there at Hollister on the Fourth of July, 1947. He was a founding member of the Boozefighters, a ringleader on two wheels. He remembers the events that created the myth and calls it all a hoax.

Cameron spent the best years of his life aboard a motorcycle. In a 1995 videotaped interview with motorcycle historian Paul Johnson, he read his resume: "I been riding motorcycles since 1928. I've had pretty near Harleys all my life—except one Crocker, which is the only bike I bought new, and I still have it."

The Boozefighters were not exactly a knitting circle, but on the

1970 TRIUMPH BONNEVILLE T120R

The Bonneville was the ultimate vertical-twin Triumph and the epitome of British bikes. Making its debut in 1959 as a twin-cylinder version of the T110 Tiger, the Bonneville remained in Triumph's lineup until 1983, by which time it had gone through numerous permutations, including the Silver Jubilee, Executive, and Royal models. The best were the basic models that weighed the least and went the fastest. Owner: John Bawoll.

1970 TRIUMPH T120R BONNEVILLE

Owner John Bawoll: "I have to admit that I like anything with wheels but I'm especially attracted to certain high-performance cars and motorcycles. So when I decided I wanted to restore a bike, it was important to me to find just the right one. Since riding was my primary goal, there were lots of good performers to consider, but I knew that something as common as a 1980s Japanese machine just wouldn't do. My choice would have to reflect my interest in the 'muscle era.' What I wanted was a sport bike that would be a good mate to my 1969 Firebird 400, and I found it in this 1970 Triumph Bonneville. Once extremely popular in North America, this model is now one of the most-sought-after British classics.

"When I first laid eyes on this Bonneville, its condition was a little rough but I could see it had great potential. At first, I just gave it a quick spray-bomb treatment so it didn't look quite so tatty, but a year later I jumped into the process of a proper in-depth restoration.

"Even though I'm mostly a purist, I couldn't resist a couple of minor changes to improve the enjoyment of riding and to personalize the Bonneville's appearance. I installed flat Vincent-style handlebars to give the bike that 'ears-back look' and put on wider-than-stock tires. I also replaced the stock rear fender stay with an earlier one to give the bike a cleaner look.

"This bike starts first kick and never ceases to amaze me when I engage first gear and roll on the throttle. The sound of the engine's throaty lope and the overall flexibility of the machine impress me on every ride.

"I once read somewhere that every car enthusiast should have a sporting British twin in the garage. How could I not agree with that?"

1960 Triumph Tiger T110

Marlon Brando rode a Triumph Thunderbird in The Wild One, *but the exact model mattered less than the fact that the motorcycle was a Triumph. The aura rubbed off on all Triumphs, and the mixture of classic British styling, a beautiful engine note, and ready speed made them the perfect machine for leather-jacketed anti-heroes everywhere. The 649-cc T110 Tiger was basically a single-carburetor Bonneville, which was OK as the Amal Monobloc was notoriously tough to tune and one was often enough. Owner: Fraser Wilson.*

other hand they weren't overgrown Boy Scouts that had turned world-class delinquents either. In Cameron's mind, they were a bunch of good old boys who liked beer and bikes, just like members of the other motorcycle clubs starting up around that same time in California—the 13 Rebels, Yellow Jackets, Galloping Gooses, Hell's Angels. Most of them were former servicemen who were drawing $20 a week for the first year out of the service—the so-called 52/20 benefit—and they were eager to taste some of the freedom they had been fighting for. But as another Boozefighter said, "We never tried to hurt anybody, because we'd all been hurt in the war. Believe me, baby, all of us had suffered in that war."

Cameron related the origin of the Boozefighters: "You've heard of 'Wino Willie'?" he starts in his best grandpa-telling-a-fairy-tale-to-grandchildren voice. "He was a good friend of mine." One day, just after World War II had ended, Wino Willie Forkner, Cameron, and some other buddies were spectating at a Class C race at El Cajon, California. "We were out in the parking lot, and that crazy Willie said, 'Let's put on a show!'

"Willie went riding right through the crash wall during intermission. The flag man tried to wave him off, but Willie ran right by him," Cameron related, a happy, misty-eyed look coming into his eyes. Astride his Indian Chief, Willie roared off down the straightaway at full throttle in full view of the abhorring crowd. "I thought he wasn't going to make that turn because I knew he was drunk," Cameron said. Lo and behold, Willie made the turn and blasted around the track for another lap—until he augered in while careening through another turn. "He tried to get back up again, but I ran out and pulled the two spark plug wires off his bike.

"Then here comes the law, and Willie went to jail," Cameron continued.

Willie was let loose again in ninety days, and that's when the Boozefighters got kickstarted.

"Willie belonged to a club called the 13 Rebels," said Cameron. "He went to a club meeting [after he got out of jail], and they jumped all over him about what he done. So he ripped his sweater off and quit."

Cameron and his bunch were having a beer at their chosen corner of heaven, the All American Bar in South Los Angeles, when the rebellious Willie walked in, stripped of his 13 Rebels colors. "We were sitting there drinking a little," remembered Cameron, "and Willie said we should start our own club." Someone retorted, "Yeah, but what'll we call it?" Another, well-oiled motorcyclist named Walt Porter drawled out, "Call it the Booozefighters: That's what they're mad about, your boozing and fighting."

It had a certain ring to it. Boozefighters it was.

On the other hand, the name was not exactly custom-made for public relations value, as Cameron remembered: "When that name came out, boy, we was nothing. Other clubs really looked down upon us."

Alongside Wino Willie, Cameron, and the veteran drinker, the Boozefighters were primarily made up of racers. Among the racers were two brothers, Ernie and John Roccio, who would become champion Class A speedway riders in Europe. In the 1950s, the Boozefighters collaborated to build "The Brute," a tuned Harley that peaked at 227 mph (365 kph) on the Bonneville Salt Flats, ridden at different times by Bobby Kelton and Jim Hunter. Meanwhile, Cameron's brother, Jim, won the grueling Big Bear Run desert race. Cameron himself ran TTs, scrambles, and anything else where he was allowed to twist his throttle wide open. Their uniform was a white sweater with green sleeves, a far cry from Brando's black leather jacket.

On the 1947 Fourth of July weekend, the Boozefighters made up their minds to hit the road. With visions dancing in their heads of motorcycle races followed by a cold beer, they rode north out of San Diego, bedrolls strapped to the back of their bikes. The sleepy little town of Hollister appeared before them like an oasis on the never-ending highway, so they turned into town and made a beeline for the local watering hole.

"All that mess never happened," Cameron said, shaking his head at memories of the *Life* photograph and *The Wild One*. On the other hand, just as Marlon Brando would say in the movie, it wasn't exactly a picnic outing, either. "Nothing happened that didn't happen at other meets," Cameron continued. "We drank a lot, maybe someone rode their motorcycle into a bar, stuff like that."

Reports differ dramatically about the number of bikers that descended on Hollister and the subsequent goings on. Some say there were upwards of 4,000 motorcyclists swarming through town, racing in the Independence Day hillclimb and scrambles, drag racing down main street, and doing everything from pioneering the art of riding motorcycles through crowded bars to razzing the vestal virgin baton-twirlers in the Independence Day parade.

News of the escapades spread, and somehow a photo was snapped that made the Boozefighters—and all cyclists everywhere—infamous.

"The war was over and *Life* magazine didn't have anything exciting," Cameron recounts, "and so they imported those people [to set up that photograph].

"It was an actor. He looked like a Boozefighter named 'Fat Boy' Nelson, but it wasn't him because Fat Boy was riding a Crocker at that time [and the guy in the photo was on a Harley]."

Still, that pictured Harley had the words "Boozefighters MC" painted across its tank.

"No one was going to sit on their bike on the sidewalk and drink that many beers; the cops would run you off," Cameron shook his head and said with the voice of experience. "You *could* do a one-time thing like ride into a bar and then ride out again."

Whatever the truth was, the photo spoke louder than the words of a handful of Boozefighters. Cameron acknowledged the effect it had with a sorrowful shake of his head:

I ride a GS with my hair so neat
Wear a war-torn parka in the
wind and sleet
—The Who,
"The Punk Meets the Godfather,"
Quadrophenia

1971 VELOCETTE VENOM THRUXTON

In North America, Velocettes were often spoken of in reverential terms as a quintessentially British motorcycle. They were rare machines that required—and earned—devotion from their owners. The Venom was a 499-cc thumper with an engine note that was music to a true biker's ears. The production racer version was named the Thruxton, as the Venoms had won many 500-cc races at the Thruxton track in England. With 40 hp on tap, the Thruxton version easily reached 105 mph (169 kph). Owner: John Oland.

"That photograph changed the image of motorcycling forever. It was one of the most important things that happened to motorcycling in all eternity. That brought on the Hell's Angels and everything else. They said, 'We'll cash in on this. We'll be the bad guys.' And that started them, and it's a doggone shame."

MEET THE HELL'S ANGELS

On Labor Day weekend 1964, the Hell's Angels held a little party. On a beach near Big Sur, California, the Angels circled their cycles, lit a campfire, and proceeded to enjoy themselves. Two wide-eyed local teenage girls happened upon the midnight festivities, only to escape to the police at dawn with cries of rape. Suddenly, the Hell's Angels were big news.

It was Hollister all over again, only worse. Shocked news media around the country shouted for justice as law-abiding citizens barred their doors and hid their daughters. Any motorcyclist, whether riding a bobbed Harley Panhead or a Whizzer, was viewed as a menace. Ever vigilant, the California attorney general issued a report on an in-depth investigation of America's new arch public enemy number one: Among the findings, the investigators reported that many of the Hell's Angels "seem badly in need of a bath."

As with many media sensations, facts about the Labor Day Hell's Angels gang rape had collided head on with fiction. The girls later admitted that they made up their story, but the image stuck: The Hell's Angels needed a bath, literally and figuratively.

The Angels were born like the Boozefighters before them as a motorcycling club made up of former service-men tasting freedom after World War II. According to one legend, the name came from the founding fathers' former army group: They had been members of the U.S. Army Air Force's 303rd Bombardment Group (H) of the famed "Mighty Eighth" Air Force that had earned its wings bombing Hitler's heartland. The 303rd took its group moniker from its most famous B-17 Flying Fortress bomber, which bore the nose-art nickname "Hell's Angels." The source of the name was credited to one crewman who reportedly exclaimed during a bomb-ing mission, "This is the closest to Hell that angels will ever get."

Like the Boozefighters, the early Angels liked to race cycles and quaff beers. In the years after the Hollister brouhaha, their image grew along with their disaffection from society. Based in the San Francisco–Oakland Bay Area, they became seen as the modern-day equivalent of the men in black hats in a horse opera. They were outlaws. Outside scattered news reports of rape and pillage, the first meeting the normal citizen had with the Hell's Angels came by way of an odd book penned by a then-unknown writer with the unlikely name of Hunter S. Thompson. Born and raised in Louisville, Kentucky, the quixotic Thompson was a down-and-out freelance journalist when he

1938 VELOCETTE BROCHURE

1975 BMW R90S

When it arrived on the scene in 1973, BMW's R90S proved two points: First, it served notice that the staid BMW firm could indeed build a sporting motorcycle. Second, it showed the rest of the sports bike makers that quality and speed were not mutually exclusive. The R90S boasted double disc front brakes, an 898-cc overhead-valve flat twin engine, 67 hp, a five-speed gearbox, and a 125-mph (200-kph) top speed. The styling, fairing, and bump-stop seat inspired many imitators. Owner: Brock Downey.

1975 BMW R90S

Owner Brock Downey: "The electric starter quickly brings the flat twin to life and I'm on my way. I like to feel the rush of that low-end grunt when I urge the machine to stretch its legs. It pulls like a husky on a leash as we cut through urban traffic.

"Once out on the highway, the R90S is a dream to ride as it devours one stretch of asphalt after another. It accelerates effortlessly and is capable of a blistering pace whenever I'm feeling a bit aggressive.

"I always keep my motorcycles in stock condition, but back in the 1970s the R90S was the kind of machine some owners would upgrade with high-performance parts because they wanted to inject extra thrills into road travel or compete at the racetrack. For me though, this bike is plenty gutsy just as it is.

"The big gas tank makes the R90S a great choice for long-distance touring, but I'm especially encouraged by the bike's reliability and comfort, and the reassurance I get from its fine craftsmanship.

"When the R90S was unveiled in late 1973, I recall thinking the silver-smoke color treatment was a tad radical for BMW, as was the bikini-style fairing. But the new look appealed to me and thousands of others. A total of 17,455 units sold between then and '76, in spite of its price being about $3,400—quite a healthy sum compared to other makes! Even though I knew about BMW's top-notch reputation, it sure seemed like a pile of money back then. So I waited a few years and picked up this nice one for a price I could handle.

"Although not a rocket by today's standards, this motorcycle still gives me endless enjoyment."

1982 HONDA CB1100R
Honda's CB1100R production racer was a development of the CB900, boasting a 1,062-cc inline four. Power was a wheel-spinning 115 hp, making the large bike nearly invincible in long-distance endurance and production races. Only a handful were produced. Owner: Byron Reynolds.

was contracted by the *Nation* magazine in 1965 to write an exposé of the Angels. His magazine piece became the basis for the book, *Hell's Angels: A Strange and Terrible Saga.*

Thompson had no fear about getting to know the Angels. In fact, he admired them. "In first meeting the Angels, at the bar of the dilapidated DePau Hotel in San Francisco, Thompson wore a Palm Beach madras-plaid sports jacket, and looked like an aluminum-siding salesman from Terre Haute," wrote his biographer, Peter O. Whitmer in *When the Going Gets Weird.* "The Angels were impressed by his brazenness, his interest in them as a group who had gotten a bad publicity rap, and by Thompson's prodigious capacity for alcohol. The first night he showed up to play pool at the DePau, they all ended up back at Hunter and Sandy's [his wife] apartment at 318 Parnassus Avenue, with the last Angel jump-starting his Harley, much to the neighbors' distaste, at 6:30 A.M., and roaring with a deafening blast up the hill and into the fog. It was a scene to be repeated innumerable times for the next year." Thompson spent his meager book advance on paying his long-in-arrears rent and buying a BSA 650 Lightning so he could ride with the gang.

Thompson became the Margaret Mead of outlaw bikers. He was shocked at the half-truths and lies that were taken for fact by the police, the courts, and citizens. He set out to right—or at least, write about—the wrongs. His book was half apologia, half peep show into the weird, wild world of the Angels. It glorified them and at the same time reviled them. He wrote, "The concept of the 'motorcycle outlaw' was as uniquely American as jazz."

It was the dawn of Thompson's brand of gonzo journalism— journalistic writing that knew there was no such thing as objectivity and so went to the other extreme of subjectivity, offering the writer's feelings, reactions, and fears front and center. His books would give a

The Hell's Angels were never good for motorcycling. Just because they ride motorcycles does not make them men.
—Evel Knievel

1990 KAWASAKI NINJA ZX11

ABOVE: *Few motorcycles were as well named as Kawasaki's Ninja—a name that fit the machine and its capabilities as well as inspiring legions of buyers. This ZX11 boasted a 1,052-cc inline four-cylinder engine with double overhead cams and sixteen valves. With power fed to the road through a six-speed gearbox, top speed was a heart-jolting 120 mph (190 kph). Owner: Herb Kriese.*

1983 DUCATI MHR

LEFT: *Hero rider Mike Hailwood's comeback victory at the 1978 Isle of Man Formula One Tourist Trophy race was the stuff of legends for Ducatisti. It was thus little wonder that Ducati would offer in 1979 a Mike Hailwood Replica based on the 900SS but dressed up in bodywork and paint mirroring Hailwood's race winner. The MHR was powered by a 864-cc version of Ingegnere Fabio Taglioni's famous desmodromic V-twin with bevel drive to the overhead camshafts. In 1985, the MHR Mille was introduced with a 973-cc engine. It lasted in production until 1986, when the Castiglioni brothers' Cagiva took control of Ducati. Owner: Ken Robertson.*

He reached for her hand and he gave her the keys
He said, I don't have any further use for these
I see angels on Ariels in leather and chrome
Swooping down from Heaven to carry me home
He gave her one last kiss and died
And he gave her his Vincent to ride.
—Richard Thompson, "1952 Vincent Black Lightning"

modern spin to theologian Søren Kierkegaard's metaphysical meditations, *Fear and Trembling*; Thompson's would carry the calling card "Fear and Loathing."

For all its faults, Thompson's *Hell's Angels* was a brilliant book. It was a journey into the heart of darkness, a Conradian tale of a journalist wowed and wooed into the ranks of the Angels. When the Angels learned that Thompson was not going to share the millions in royalties that they expected him to earn with their story, they "stomped" him. Only the intervention of one Angel known as Tiny saved his life. Thompson jumped in his car and drove away, quoting Conrad's Kurtz: "The horror . . . the horror."

Thompson's *Hell's Angels* hit the bestseller charts on its release in 1967 and sold out its small first printing in a flash. Suddenly, the Angels were a subject of fascination, the dark side of society now illuminated by Thompson's gonzo ethnography. A wave of biker chic soon followed. The fashion world fell in love with black leather jackets and pants and motorcycle-chain belts; coffee-table photography books and lurid potboiler biker magazines filled the shelves; and a whole slew of Hell's Angels B-budget movies, featuring the Angels starring as themselves, hit the drive-in theaters to horrify and titillate the masses. Several of the Hell's Angels even began to write their own memoirs, including "Freewheelin'" Frank Reynolds's *Secretary of the Angels*, and the high-profile Angels president Sonny Barger appeared on television talk shows, magazine covers, and anywhere else he could promote himself. The Hell's Angels were the next big thing.

THE ENDURING MYTH OF THE OUTLAW BIKER MYSTIQUE

Today, the Hell's Angels have their own Internet website. The town of Hollister holds an annual Independence Day motorcycle race and rally, trading on the commercial value of the 1947 fracas that was once seen as threatening the end of the free world as we know it. Black leather motorcycle jackets are as common as boxer shorts, and if you're a stockbroker or dentist that *doesn't* own a Harley, you stand out from the crowd. Hunter S. Thompson's *Hell's Angels* is now in its thirtysomething printing and is shelved in bookstores in the staid Sociology section. *The Wild One*, once the scourge of movie theaters, is a popular video rental and timepiece, dated fifties chic. Getting on the waiting list to buy a Harley and riding to the "biker" rallies at Sturgis, South Dakota, or Daytona, Florida, is all part and parcel of your everyday mid-life crisis.

The motorcycle has come full circle in acceptance. The outlaw biker mystique that once shocked and terrified the masses has been subjugated into the mainstream, eaten up by society, and spit out as everyday fashion.

THE SHRINER CONNECTION

No one loves motorcycles more than Shriners. Who hasn't been stunned by a Shriner Motor Corps's dazzling riding skills, intricate death-defying figure-eight maneuvers, and devil-may-care roundabouts at a Fourth of July parade? Shriners and motorcycles were made for each other.

The Shriners' love of cycles can be traced back to one man. Cushman chief Bob Ammon was a Shriner with a vision: In his mind's eye, he saw the fez-capped ones riding motorscooters in a dizzying ballet and throwing taffy to children with the grace of waving dairy princesses.

Ammon offered Cushman scooters to his brethren at a fleet price and dressed the miniature machines up in an extra helping of chrome to wow the folks on Main Street. In turn, Shriners helped keep Cushman's ledger books flowing in black ink for decades.

Naturally, sharp-eyed salespeople from other makes caught on to Cushman's gimmick and began offering Shriners fleet prices on everything from BMW flat twins to Harley-Davidson Big Twins, complete with special Shriner accessory packages.

Many Shriner Motor Corps used their cycles for only a handful of seasons; they trailered them to parades and added few miles to the odometer—most of them in figure-eights. Today, Shriner scooters and motorcycles often command big money from collectors as they are different from run-of-the-mill models, weighted down with accessories, boast low mileage, and have lived a life of loving care.

THE SHRINER CONNECTION
Cushman chief Bob Ammon was a long-standing Shriner who came up with the brilliant idea of selling scooters to his brethren to ride in local Fourth of July parades. Cushman even offered a heady list of dress-up accessories and chrome trinkets in its special Shriner package—sold to the fellow Temple members at a bargain fleet price, of course. Shriners took to scooters—and later, full-sized motorcycles—like ducks to water and created dazzling scooter ballets for adoring parade-goers everywhere.

They were a Don Quixote and a Sancho Panza for the twentieth century. A dynamic duo like Batman and Robin. Outlaws of quality like Butch Cassidy and the Sundance Kid. Or maybe they were Laurel and Hardy. In the end, they were themselves, Captain America and Billy, and through a simple, low-budget, shot-on-the-run movie called *Easy Rider*, they created a new legend.

Captain America and Billy were good bad guys. They were anti-heroes on the wrong side of an Establishment that did not understand them and their times. They were part motorcycle outlaw in the style of *The Wild One* and part modern American cowboy looking for a home on the range. They were something new, and they became cultural icons. Captain America and Billy rode their chopped Harleys off the movie screen of *Easy Rider* to inspire generations of motorcyclists on their "great American freedom machines," as Harley-Davidson advertisements would jump on the bandwagon and label them.

THE CORNIEST STORY EVER TOLD

The first of many ironies was that in *Easy Rider*, the greatest on-the-road, wind-in-the-hair, hippie-biker movie ever made, the motorcycles were built from former Los Angeles Police Department (LAPD) cruisers. Peter Fonda, a.k.a. Captain America, bought four Harley-Davidson Panheads—a 1950, two '51s, and a '52—at an LAPD auction for $500 apiece. These lackeys of the Establishment were about to become the wheels to fuel the anti-Establishment's wildest dream.

The idea for *Easy Rider* came to Fonda in a marijuana-fueled vision. It was 1967, the Summer of Love, and he was trapped at a movie exhibitors' convention in Toronto, flogging the latest biker flick that he was starring in, *The Wild Angels*, facing an endless, Kafka-esque sentence of tedious press interviews. Then, the chief of the Motion Picture Association of America stood up to harangue the audience, denouncing Fonda and his film, saying, "We should stop making movies about motorcycles, sex, and drugs, and make more motion pictures like *Doctor Doolittle.*"

Fonda finally escaped. He made it back to his red-flocked room at the Lakeshore Motel, only to be greeted by piles of promotional 8x10 glossies that required his autograph. Unable to face the promotion routine, he drank a couple bottles of Heineken and smoked a joint. As the marijuana settled his mind, he gazed at one of the photographs, which showed him and co-star Bruce Dern on a chopper. The vision came to him.

"I understood immediately just what kind of motorcycle, sex, and drugs movie I should make next," he wrote thirty years later in his autobiography, *Don't Tell Dad*. The movie, which he originally planned to title *The Loners*, would be the modern Western: Two cool cats would take off on their choppers in search of America. They had just made a big drug score and were riding across the country to retire in Florida, when a couple of duck poachers in a truck gun them down because they didn't like the way they looked.

Fonda was on a roll. It was 4:30 A.M., and he telephoned his best friend and biggest enemy, Dennis Hopper, got him out of bed, and told him the story. Hopper was ready to go.

Then Fonda told the idea to his wife. Her response was straightforward enough: "That's the corniest story I've ever heard."

MONKEE MONEY

The second irony was that Hollywood—or at least the semi-underground, low-rent, youth-exploitation side of the movie industry—was ready to ride with Fonda's dream. With the help of novelist and screenwriter Terry Southern, Fonda and Hopper put together an audiotape of Hopper describing the storyline, and they set out to pitch it. After a deal fell through with American International Pictures, the champion of biker flicks up to that time, Fonda was turned on to two producers, Bert Schneider and Bob Rafelson, who had struck gold with the faux-Beatles TV "rock group" The Monkees. The producers dug the concept. There and then, they wrote out a check for $40,000 to start things rolling. As Fonda noted in his autobiography, "Monkee money made *Easy Rider*."

Fonda then took a portion of the grubstake to the LAPD auction and bought the four Panheads. With the help of some buddies, the cycles were rebuilt in a manner far from Milwaukee's or the police department's concept. "I'd designed the extended and mildly raked front forks, helmet, sissy bar, and the tank," Fonda wrote, "but the forty-two degree rake that was suggested by [black activist and some-

1973 TRIUMPH X75 HURRICANE
The chopper craze inspired many formerly sane motorcycle designers to recast their suddenly boring machines as "customs." Triumph hired California's Craig Vetter to make its Trident triple hip. The forks were subtly raked, the seat shortened, the handlebars lengthened, and swept-back exhausts were added to create the Hurricane. The model lasted but one season. Owner: Rick Martens.

times motorcycle customizer] Cliff Vaughs was some piece of work."

As soon as his cycle was ready, Fonda took to the road to get the hang of riding a chopper. "I began riding the L.A. freeway system," remembered Fonda. "I was stopped every night by the police. They measured my handlebars, measured the height of the headlight, checked the taillights, the registration. They didn't touch the throttle."

Choppers were a new scene, but after the Captain America motorcycle rolled across movie screens around the world, they would become the rage. In garages everywhere, ersatz Captain Americas were soon hurriedly chopping their cycles, raking the forks, throwing away perfectly good but out-of-fashion parts, and painting American flags on any surface large enough to hold the stars and stripes.

IN THE SPIRIT OF MUSSOLINI

The third irony was that filming and production of the ultimate anti-Establishment road movie approached the workings of a fascist state.

"Dennis started with a bang," Fonda remembered. In lieu of a pep talk, Hopper led off the first day of filming in New Orleans with a Mussolini-esque rant to tell everyone that this was his movie and they all better follow orders.

They began filming by shooting from the hip in the best cowboy tradition, a technique that was ideal for the making of this modern Western. Fonda and Hopper knew what they wanted to capture on film but they eschewed the convention of a script, although there were numerous attempts to write one with the help of Terry Southern. Instead, they just started the cameras rolling.

They filmed in New Orleans during Mardi Gras, before the motorcycles were ready. They wanted to capture an LSD trip on film, so they shot Captain America, Billy, and a bevy of girl groupies in a cemetery waxing poetic on things that made metaphysical sense to them at the time.

After several rounds of fights between Hopper and most of the rest of the crew, the people who hadn't quit returned to Los Angeles. Fonda and Hopper fired up the cycles, and they began filming as they rode across the United States.

Easy Rider was true *cinema verité*. They planned some scenes ahead of time, got set up, and then let things unfold as the camera shot their improvisations. One campfire conversation was inspired half by marijuana and half by their feel for the times:

The Lawyer (Jack Nicholson): "They're not scared of you. They're scared of what you represent to them."

Billy (Dennis Hopper): "Hey man, all we represent to them, man, is someone who needs a haircut."

The Lawyer: "Oh no, what you represent to them is freedom."

Billy: "What the hell's wrong with freedom? Man, that's what it's all about."

The Lawyer: "Oh yeah, that's right, that's what it's all about all right. But talking about it and doing it, that's two different things. I

We seemed to breathe more freely, a lighter air, an air of adventure.
—Che Guevara,
The Motorcycle Diaries

mean, it's real hard to be free when you are bought and sold in the marketplace. But don't ever tell anybody that they're not free because then they gonna get real busy killing and maiming to prove to you that they are. Oh yeah, they gonna talk to you and talk to you and talk to you about individual freedom, but when they see a free individual, it's gonna scare 'em."

Other times, serendipity was the director. On one occasion, the crew arrived at a restaurant in Morganza, Louisiana, to film a scene where locals harass the bikers only to run into a group of true locals that actually did harass them. Fonda remembered their taunts: "I kin smell 'em!" one local said about the grungy bikers, who just happened to be the director and producer of the film, "Kin yew smell 'em? I kin smell 'em!" Fonda and Hopper enlisted them in the movie, and they repeated everything they had just said, this time with the camera rolling. One of the locals turned out to be a deputy sheriff, pleased to play a role in a real Hollywood movie.

RIDING INTO THE SUNSET

The final—and ongoing—irony is that the movie made big money, money that is still contested between many of the principals in the production of the film. The film cost $501,000 to make, and according to Hopper, "We made all of our money back the first week. In one theater."

The time was right for *Easy Rider* when it finally rode onto the movie screen, and it was no irony that the film made it big. As Hopper recollected later, "Nobody had ever seen themselves portrayed in a movie. At every love-in across the country people were smoking grass and dropping LSD, while audiences were still watching Doris Day and Rock Hudson."

From the start, Fonda and Hopper knew they had a good thing, and they demanded a share of the profits, 11 percentage points each of the take. And somewhere along the road, this film about down-and-out drifters made Fonda and Hopper millionaires.

It also inspired ongoing legal wrangling between the movie's principals as to who owns the legend. Fonda, Hopper, and Terry Southern have battled for decades now over who authored the script—such as it was. In 1995, Hopper sued Fonda for a larger cut of movie profits. Not happy with the 33 percent of the proceeds he has earned, Hopper wanted 41 percent of the $40 million to $70 million that the movie was estimated to have made since its debut. The legal battles continued.

But the story of *Easy Rider* did not end when Captain America and Billy were gunned down by rednecks in a pickup truck along a nameless stretch of road somewhere in the middle of America. Like the gas that fueled Captain America's chopper, the movie fueled an image of the motorcycle as the Great American Freedom Machine that lives on today as strong as ever.

The Buddha, the Godhead, resides quite as comfortably in the circuits of a digital computer or the gears of a cycle transmission as he does at the top of a mountain or in the petals of a flower.
—Robert M. Pirsig,
Zen and the Art of Motorcycle Maintenance, 1974

Chapter 9

THE
SOUND HEARD
AROUND THE WORLD

BACK TO THE FUTURE

1983 HARLEY-DAVIDSON XR1000

ABOVE: *Ironically, some of the models considered in retrospect to be among Harley-Davidson's best were machines that didn't sell when new. The XLCR café racer proved the point, as did the XR1000. Created as an XR750 racer for the street, the XR1000 was a thoroughbred hot rod. Its tuned 998-cc engine boasted trick cylinder heads and dual Dell'Orto carburetors sourced from the XR. In standard tune, it put out 70 hp at 6,000 rpm, rocketing the 470-pound (213-kg) sled to a top speed of 120 mph (193 kph). Owner: Jim Wild.*

1993 HARLEY-DAVIDSON FLSTN "MOO-GLIDE"

LEFT: *In 1993, Milwaukee offered this special edition model with the ungainly name of FLSTN Heritage Softail Nostalgia. Coming from Wisconsin, the styling was bovine based, with its Holstein-inspired black-and-white paint scheme and cowhide inserts on the saddlebags, seat, and pillion. The model soon earned the more descriptive moniker "Moo-Glide." Owner: Jim Ference.*

It was a sound heard around the world. Kicking over their first engine in 1901, William S. Harley and Arthur Davidson unwittingly created the foundation of the empire that would become Harley-Davidson, Inc. When that first single-cylinder engine evolved into the duo's premier V-twin of 1909, the sound was echoed by the second cylinder.

The V-twin engine architecture became the trunk of the company's family tree. Harley-Davidson branched out into experimenting with an opposed twin, other single configurations, two-strokes, and more, but Milwaukee always remained true to that V-twin. Through the years, the V-twin grew into a side-valve motor, then into the famous overhead-cam Knucklehead, Panhead, and Shovelhead before evolving into the aptly-named V^2 Evolution and in turn, its evolution, the new Twin Cam 88. Due to the shapes of their mechanical sculpture, some wags nicknamed the Evolution the "Blockhead" and dubbed the new Twin Cam 88 the "Fathead."

Ever proud of its legacy and ever vigilant of its property, Harley-Davidson filed with the U.S. Patent and Trademark Office (PTO) on February 1, 1994, to register the sound of its V-twin engine as a trademark. As the application read: "The [trade]mark consists of the exhaust sound of applicant's motorcycles, produced by V-twin, common crankpin motorcycle engines when the goods are in use."

The sound heard around the world was to be legally protected.

THE SOUND AND THE FURY

Ironically, in the years when Harley and Davidson were kickstarting their company to life, Arthur Davidson was concerned about the loud noise Bill Harley's newfangled engine made. Many ordinary folk who were not fascinated by the "infernal-combustion" engine had nothing but curses to shower on it, rather than the expected praise. The world was simply a quieter place back then, and terrifying horses with backfires was not a great publicity stunt for the fledgling Motor Company. So, as legend has it, Arthur Davidson asked Bill Harley if he could tone that thing down: Loud pipes were costing sales. As chief engineer, Harley experimented with various exhaust pipes and mufflers to make the note of the firm's motorcycles sound like music to the ears.

The sonority of the Harley-Davidson V-twin drew praises over the years—albeit from motorcycling journalists rather than opera divas. Harley-Davidson Archivist Dr. Martin Jack Rosenblum searched company records for mention of the engine's sound as part of preparing the firm's trademark

1997 BUELL S1 LIGHTNING

Erik Buell sometimes felt himself to be a fish out of water. He was a Harley-Davidson employee with a taste for sporting motorcycles, which seemed like a dramatic contradiction as Harley-Davidson had a corner on the North American cruiser market. At the dawn of the 1980s, Buell left Harley and set up his own sportbike-building firm with the Motor Company's blessing. Early Buells were powered by Sportster engines fitted into a multi-tube frame, but demand for a Harley-powered road rocket was unfortunately limited. In 1993, Harley took a stronger interest in Buell's project, and together they formed a new Buell company. The resulting Buell S1 Lightning was powered by a highly tuned 1,203-cc Harley V-twin and won rave reviews from a new breed of Harley fans. Owner: Harley-Davidson of Southern Alberta.

registration: "I looked through the archives for any mention of the sound of the V-twin engine," Rosenblum said. "I began in 1909, and found ample references, more than you'd imagine. This was the outside world responding [to the Harley engine's note], motorcycle magazines describing it as charactertisic and unique even way back then."

Harley-Davidson is far from the first American company to seek to trademark a sound, according to attorney Michael B. Sapherstein. Aural trademarks granted by the PTO include the MGM lion's roar and the Harlem Globetrotters basketball team's trademarked song, "Sweet Georgia Brown." The precedent for trademarked sounds was set in 1950 by the National Broadcasting Company (NBC) when it registered the musical notes G, E, and C played on chimes as a trademark for its radio broadcasts. A sound may not be the most bizarre trademark, either. Scents and fragrances have been registered to distinguish products, and color has been ruled acceptable for trademark application. Still, the PTO reports that only 23 of the more than 729,000 registered trademarks in the United States are sounds.

Naturally, when Harley-Davidson applied for its aural trademark, it needed to describe the engine sound to help the PTO determine if the trademark could be protected if granted. A cassette tape of an Evolution V-twin accompanied the application, but describing the sound in mere words was tough.

A musician might explain it as "syncopated." A non-motorcyclist would probably simply complain that it was "loud." Ducati riders, astride their own V-twins, may term it "uneducated." Harley aficionados often claim they can pick out a Harley with their eyes closed. And Harley's own trademark attorney, Joseph Bonk, compared the sound to the unpretentious spud, stating that the engine design results in a loping idle that sounds like "*potato–potato–potato.*"

THE SOUND OF THE TIMES

Harley-Davidson's trademark application drew everything from guffaws to outrage. But the legal chess move was not mere corporate bullying, as some folk saw it.

In these days of retro chic, it should come as little surprise that Harley-Davidson sought to protect its sound: The Motor Company heard that sweet engine note as an essential element of its history and image. Tim Hoelter, Harley-Davidson's vice president and general counsel, explained the application: "We've been designing, manufacturing, and selling our motorcycles with the unique Harley-Davidson sound for decades in the United States, but our competitors have not been—and in fact they have made fun of us for maintaining the tradition and heritage that is so interwoven within our brand."

And therein lay the crux of the situation. The tradition and heritage of the Harley V-twin's sound could be measured not only in decibels but also in dollars and cents.

After ruling the roost for decades, Harley-Davidson's home market share was slowly but surely gouged away by foreign motorcycle makes

1997 Triumph Daytona T595

ABOVE: *The resurrection of Triumph in 1991 was greeted with grave skepticism among the faithful. After all, the original firm had died a protracted and ignominious death. But the new machines were well developed and lived up to every promise, winning back former Triumph riders and bringing a new generation to the fold. The T595 Daytona was powered by a fuel-injected 955-cc inline triple. Owner: Jim Wild.*

1997 Ducati 916SPS

LEFT: *After decades as an underdog, Ducati finally ruled the sportbike world starting in the late 1980s due to cutting edge Italian engineering and styling as well as a solid financial foundation from the United States. Upon its introduction in 1995, the exalted 916 established the Borgo Panigale firm as a maker of truly exotic machinery that could also win races. The 916 was powered by a 916-cc double-overhead-cam desmodromic V-twin. It was tough to imagine a more stunning motorcycle. Owner: Ken Robertson.*

starting in the 1950s. By the 1980s, the North American motorcycle market was dominated by the Japanese Big Three: Honda, Yamaha, and Suzuki. Harley-Davidson was fighting to pull itself up by its bootstraps, and it needed all the help it could get. In the 1990s, the company resurrected itself—and it doesn't want to lose ground again. Harley-Davidson's greatest asset is its history, and it has served notice that it will fight to protect that tradition and heritage.

1992 MOTO GUZZI DAYTONA 1000

Throughout the 1980s, the venerable Moto Guzzi firm was running on effete engineering that dated back to the first V7 of 1967. New inspiration, however, arrived from an unlikely source: American dentist Dr. John Wittner, who had a way with tuning Guzzis for the racetrack. Wittner's race wins helped rejuvenate Guzzi's spirit, and along with new funding and engineering, the revived company unveiled new models throughout the 1990s. The Daytona 1000 was based on Dr. John's race winner and featured the Weber Marelli electronic fuel injection feeding its 992-cc 90-degree V-twin. Weighing a hefty 447 pounds (205 kg), the Daytona was good for 153 mph (245 kph). Owner: Brian Taylor.

Harley's situation was not unique. Similar scenarios were played out around the globe in the 1990s as other vaunted marques sought to re-establish themselves—and each carried a tradition and heritage that they too sought to protect and prolong.

In Italy, Ducati was reasserting itself after numerous financial tribulations. Like Harley, Ducati had built a reputation with its V-twins, although Ducati's cylinders were splayed at 90 degrees. Moto Guzzi was struggling but found new financial backing and rejuvenated its transverse V-twin. And the great MV Agusta was back as well, with a new inline four and bodywork painted in the instantly identifiable colors of fire-engine red and silver.

In England, Triumph made a resurgence and won praise for its new generation of machines that bore new mechanical specifications but wore glorious old names. Norton too made promises of a resurrection. Even Excelsior-Henderson in the United States had tried to make a return. These companies all looked back to their legacy in charting a path to their future, and big money was spent in getting their engines to sound "right."

In its own V-twin engine, Harley-Davidson heard the sound of its own history and mystique: the first note of the premier Harley-Davidsons born in a shed, the sound of the Wrecking Crew beating Indian to the checkered flag, the bravado of Lee Marvin in *The Wild One*, the coolness of Peter Fonda in *Easy Rider*, the roar of Evel Knievel, and the siren call of the open road.

BIBLIOGRAPHY

Bachman, Scott, et. al. *Evel★Ways: The Attitude of Evel Knievel.* Minneapolis, Minnesota: GraF/X, 1999.

Biskind, Peter. *Easy Riders, Raging Bulls: How the Sex-Drugs-and-Rock'n'Roll Generation Saved Hollywood.* New York: Simon & Schuster, 1998.

Bolfert, Thomas C. *The Big Book of Harley-Davidson.* Milwaukee, Wisconsin: Harley-Davidson, Inc., 1991.

Brando, Marlon, with Robert Lindsey. *Songs My Mother Taught Me.* New York: Random House, 1994.

Brooke, Lindsay, and David Gaylin. *Triumph Motorcycles in America.* Osceola, Wisconsin: Motorbooks International, 1993.

Collins, Ace. *Evel Knievel: An American Hero.* New York: St. Martin's Press, 1999.

Dregni, Eric. "The Rebel and Harley-Davidson." Unpublished paper. 1994.

Dregni, Michael, and Eric Dregni. *Scooters!* Osceola, Wisconsin: Motorbooks International, 1995.

Duffield, J. W. *Bert Wilson's Twin Cylinder Racer.* Racine, Wisconsin: Western Printing & Lithography Co., 1924. Copyright 1914.

Dumas, François-Marie, and Didier Ganneau. *Scooters du Monde: 100 ans d'histoire.* Paris: Editions EPA, 1995.

Field, Greg. *Harley-Davidson Knuckleheads.* Osceola, Wisconsin: Motorbooks International, 1997.

Fonda, Peter. *Don't Tell Dad.* New York: Hyperion Press, 1998.

Girdler, Allan. "First Fired, First Forgotten." *Cycle World,* February 1998.

Girdler, Allan. "The Miller Mystery." *Cycle World,* March 1996.

Harper, Roy. *Vincent Vee-Twins.* London: Osprey Publishing, 1982.

Hatfield, Jerry. *American Racing Motorcycles.* Sparkford, England: Haynes Publishing Group, 1982.

Hatfield, Jerry. *Illustrated Antique American Motorcycle Buyer's Guide.* Osceola, Wisconsin: Motorbooks International, 1996.

Johnson, Paul "P.J." *Yesterdays Motorcycle Stars.* Twenty hours of videotaped interviews with 130 motorcycling legends collected over a period of two years. Tijeras, New Mexico: 1995.

Kassel, Michael B. "Revolution in 50cc." Website: www.ready.to.ware.com, 1996.

Leffingwell, Randy. *Harley-Davidson: Myth & Mystique.* Osceola, Wisconsin: Motorbooks International, 1995.

Lott, Lucky Lee. *The Legend of the Lucky Lee Lott Hell Drivers.* Osceola, Wisconsin: Motorbooks International, 1994.

McKeen, William. *Hunter S. Thompson.* Boston: Twayne Publishers, 1991.

McShane, Clay. *Down the Asphalt Path: The Automobile and the American City.* New York: Columbia City Press, 1994.

Miller, Zachary. *Illustrated Vincent Motorcycle Buyer's Guide.* Osceola, Wisconsin: Motorbooks International, 1994.

Oliver, Smith Hempstone, and Donald H. Berkebile. *The Smithsonian Collection of Automobiles and Motorcycles.* Washington, D. C.: Smithsonian Institution Press, 1968. Smithsonian publication 4719.

Pomerantz, Gary M. "The Daredevil Doesn't Jump Anymore But That Hasn't Stopped Him From Being Evel Knievel." *Icon,* April 1998.

Pridmore, Jay, and Jim Hurd. *Schwinn Bicycles.* Osceola, Wisconsin: Motorbooks International, 1996.

Sapherstein, Michael B. "The Trademark Registrability of the Harley-Davidson Roar: A Multimedia Analysis." Intellectual Property and Trademark Forum at Boston College Law School website: www.bc.edu/iptf, 1998.

Schilling, Phil. "Nifty Fifties." *Cycle World,* April 1999.

Schultz, Richard Henry. *Hendersons: Those Elegant Machines. The Complete History of Henderson Motorcycles (1911–1931).* Freeman, South Dakota: Pine Hill Press, Inc., 1994.

Thompson, Hunter S. *Hell's Angels: A Strange and Terrible Saga.* New York: Random House, 1967.

Thompson, Jon F. "Return of a Warhorse." *Cycle World,* January 1998.

Whitmer, Peter O. *When the Going Gets Weird: The Twisted Life and Times of Hunter S. Thompson: A Very Unauthorized Biography.* New York: Hyperion, 1993.

Wright, Stephen. *American Racer 1900–1939.* Huntington Beach, California: Megden Publishing Co., 1979.

INDEX

ABOUT THE AUTHOR AND PHOTOGRAPHER

MICHAEL DREGNI is the author of several obscure books on a variety of eclectic yet esoteric subjects. His engineering history of Ferrari automobiles, *Inside Ferrari*, was published in English, Japanese, and German. He co-authored two pop-culture histories of motorscooters and is at work on a history of Moto Parilla for an Italian publisher. He is also the author of *Harley-Davidson Collectibles*, *This Old Tractor*, *This Old Farm*, and *Minnesota Days*, all published by Voyageur Press. He currently lives in Minneapolis, Minnesota, with his wife Sigrid, sons Nico and Marco, and dog Ciccia.

The author at work. (Photograph © Randy Leffingwell)

JOHN DEAN is a freelance photographer based in Calgary, Alberta, with numerous long-term commercial clients and an eclectic list of personal photo projects. He graduated from the Alberta College of Art and Design in 1975 and was a photographer at the Glenbow Museum in Calgary before opening his own studio in 1986. He specializes in product, architectural, industrial, and fine art photographic assignments. The images in this book were photographed on 4x5 Kodak and Fuji film with a Horseman 4x5 camera, Rodenstock 210 APO Macro and 150 Nikkor lenses, Speedotron and Broncolor strobes, and Lightbrush fiber optic lighting.

John Dean